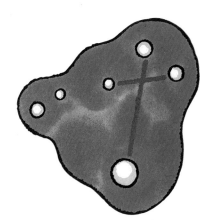

The OXFORD Children's A to Z of Space

Robin Kerrod

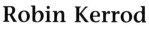

OXFORD
UNIVERSITY PRESS

Oxford University Press
Great Clarendon Street
Oxford OX2 6DP

Oxford New York
Athens Auckland Bangkok Bogotá Buenos
Aires Calcutta Cape Town Chennai Dar es
Salaam Delhi Florence Hong Kong Istambul
Karachi Kuala Lumpur Madrid Melbourne
Mexico City Mumbai Nairobi Paris São Paulo
Singapore Taipei Tokyo Toronto Warsaw
and associated companies in
Berlin Ibadan

Oxford is a registered trade mark of
Oxford University Press

Text copyright © Robin Kerrod 1999

British Library Cataloguing in Publication Data
Data available

First published 1999

ISBN 0–19–910472-7 (paperback)
ISBN 0–19–910471-9 (hardback)

10 9 8 7 6 5 4 3 2 1

Printed in Italy

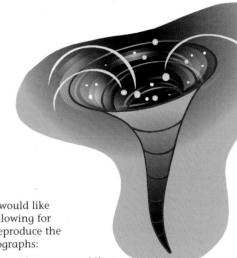

Acknowledgements

Design: Joshua Smith

Picture research:
Charlotte Lippmann

Abbreviations: t = top;
b = bottom; l = left;
r = right; c = centre;
back = background

Photographs

The publishers would like
to thank the following for
permission to reproduce the
following photographs:

Anglo-Australian Observatory: 29b

Corbis Images: 7b (Bettmann); 10l (NASA); 10tr (Paul
A. Souders);14t (Space Telescope Science Institute); 17t
(Charles & Josette Lenars); 19c (NASA); 28tr (James L.
Amos); 43cl (NASA); 63b (Joseph Sohm;
ChromoSohm Inc.)

Mary Evans Picture Library: 58tl

Fortean Picture Library: 61tl

Getty Images: 8br; 16cr; 22cr; 23tc; 32tr

Robin Kerrod: 5br; 28tl; 32cl; 34br; 41tl; 47b; 48tr; 62tl

The Lovell Radio Telescope and Science Centre at Jodrell Bank

The University of Manchester: 31bl

NASA: 4br; 6tl; 7cr; 8t; 9b; 12tr; 14-15b; 18tr; 22t and bl; 22-23 c;
24bl; 26bl; 27tl; 29tl; 30tl and r; 31cr and br; 33b; 36tr and cl;
38cl; 39b; 40tr and bl; 42br; 43bl; 44; 45; 46tl; 49t; 50-51; 52t;
55tl; 56; 57; 58tr and br; 59tl; 61tr and b; 62r

NOVOSTI (London): 12-13b

The Observatories of the Carnegie Institution of Washington: 9c

Science Photo Library: 18b (Hencoup Enterprises); 24cr; 25bl and
48tl (Space Telescope Science Institute/NASA); 35tr (US Geological
Survey); 53t and 64t (NASA)

Spacecharts Photo Library: 6br; 8bl; 15t; 16l; 17bl; 20t; 21b; 26br;
28b and background; 35cl; 37 t and b; 38b; 39t; 40tl; 46b; 49br;
50; 51r; 52b; 54t; 55r; 59bl; 64l

Illustrations and diagrams

Julian Baum front cover bl, 6, 14/15, 25r, 33, 38, 47l, 54t,
58, 63

Clive Goodyer front cover tl, 10 both, 12b, 15, 17, 19, 20 both, 27b,
32, 36, 41r, 42t, 46, 60l, 64 and planet symbols

David Hardy 7, 11b, 56, 57

John Haslam back cover tl, 5t, 12t, 18, 21, 24 25l, 27t, 29, 31, 34,
41l, 47r, 60r

Nick Hawken 4 both, 11t,13, 26, 34, 42b, 48, 49, 51, 53 both,
54b, 59

Oxford Illustrators front cover br, 35

John Walker 5b

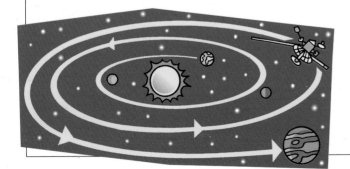

Dear Reader

Every night, if the weather is clear, you can enjoy one of the finest sights in nature – the night sky. Thousands of twinkling stars shine down out of the velvety blackness of space. Some of the bright 'stars' that you see are not stars at all, but planets. These are our neighbours in space.

If you go star-gazing often, you will learn to recognize the constellations – the patterns made by the bright stars. Then you will be well on your way to becoming an astronomer. Astronomers are scientists who study the night sky and all the objects that appear in it. Looking through powerful telescopes, they see millions more stars and great star islands, or galaxies.

The A to Z of Space explains more than 350 space words. On its pages you will find out how astronomers go about their work, and what they have discovered about the heavens. Discover how stars are born and die, what black holes are, why eclipses happen, when the Universe began – and much, much more.

This book also tells you about exploring the Universe from space, both by robot spacecraft and human astronauts. Find out what a satellite does, why rockets can work in space, and how astronauts live in space.

There is much to marvel at, and wonder about, in this exciting introduction to astronomy and space travel. Enjoy it!

Robin Kerrod

A

Achernar

See **star**.

Acrux

See **star**.

active galaxy

See **galaxy**.

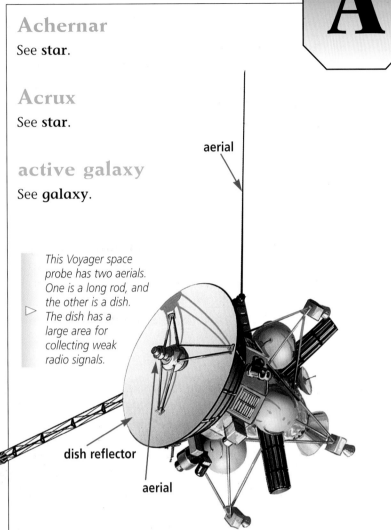

aerial

This Voyager space probe has two aerials. One is a long rod, and the other is a dish. The dish has a large area for collecting weak radio signals.

dish reflector

aerial

aerial

An aerial sends out or receives radio signals. Another word for aerial is antenna. Spacecraft have aerials to receive instructions from **mission control** on the ground, and also to send back pictures and data (information) to Earth.
See also **radio telescope**.

aerolite

An aerolite is a piece of stone from space. It is a kind of **meteorite**. Nine out of ten meteorites are aerolites.

aerospace

Aerospace is short for two words: 'aeronautics' and 'space'. Aeronautics means travel through the air. Aerospace companies design and build both aircraft and spacecraft.

air

Air is the mixture of gases that surrounds us. We breathe air all the time. The main gases in it are nitrogen and oxygen. Humans and most other living things must take in oxygen from the air to stay alive. The layers of air around the Earth form an **atmosphere**.

This pie chart shows the different amounts of the gases found in air. Oxygen, the gas we must breathe to live, makes up only about one-fifth of the air.

nitrogen

oxygen

other gases

argon

airlock

An airlock is a special area inside a spacecraft. Air can be pumped out of an airlock and then let back in again. Astronauts pass through an airlock when they leave their spacecraft to go space walking and when they return.
See also **extravehicular activity**.

Astronauts move through the airlock of the space shuttle before going on a space walk. In this picture, the airlock is depressurized (has no air in it).

air resistance

See **drag**.

Aldebaran

See **star**.

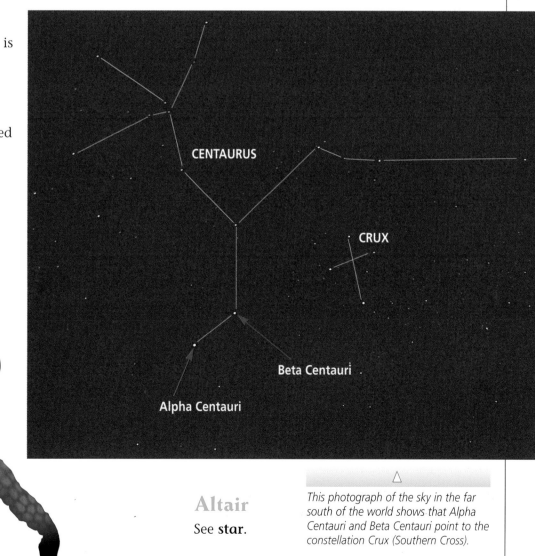

Algol is a pair of stars that circle around each other. It 'winks', or becomes dim, when the large dim star passes in front of the smaller, brighter one.

almanac

An almanac is a book that gives information about the year ahead. It includes a calendar and often information about the movements of the Sun, Moon, planets and stars. Astronomers use an almanac that gives the exact positions of certain stars at any time.

Algol

Algol is a star in the constellation Perseus. Ancient astronomers called it 'the Winking Demon'. Most of the time it shines steadily, but every few days it suddenly dims for a while. This happens because Algol is a **double star**.

Alpha Centauri

Alpha Centauri is one of the brightest stars that you can see. It is closer to Earth than any of the other bright stars in the sky. It lies about 4.3 **light-years** away. Alpha Centauri and its companion, Beta Centauri, are the brightest stars in the constellation Centaurus. See also **star**.

alien

Alien means something that is from another world out in space. Some people believe that alien creatures have landed on Earth, and some say they have been kidnapped by aliens. But there is no real proof that these stories are true. See also **life in space, SETI, UFO**.

People who claim that they have seen aliens say they look something like this. If they do exist, real aliens would probably look very different from this one.

CENTAURUS

CRUX

Beta Centauri

Alpha Centauri

Altair

See **star**.

This photograph of the sky in the far south of the world shows that Alpha Centauri and Beta Centauri point to the constellation Crux (Southern Cross).

Andromeda Galaxy

The Andromeda Galaxy appears as a misty patch in the sky. It is one of the few galaxies that you can see with the naked eye. It has the same spiral shape as the **Milky Way Galaxy**, but is much bigger.

The Andromeda Galaxy is so far away that its light takes over 2 million years to reach us.

Antares

See **star**.

antenna

See **aerial**.

Apollo spacecraft

Apollo spacecraft carried US astronauts to the Moon between 1969 and 1972. Each craft was made up of three **modules** (parts). The crew of three lived in a command module. Fuel and equipment were carried in a service module. Two crew members travelled down to the Moon's surface and back in a lunar module. See also **exploring space, Saturn V**.

The complete Apollo spacecraft measured more than 10 metres long and weighed 45 tonnes.

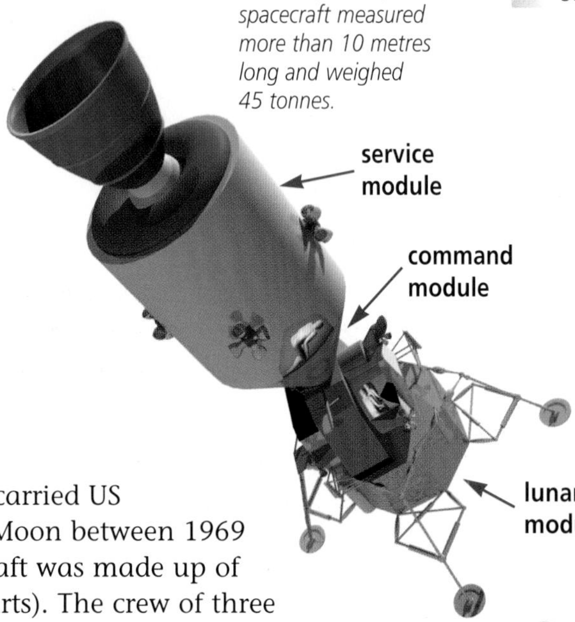

service module

command module

lunar module

Aquarius

See **zodiac**.

Arcturus

See **star**.

Ariane

Ariane is the name of a family of rockets that launch satellites. Ariane rockets are used by the European Space Agency. The main rocket used at present is *Ariane 4*, which is fitted with two or four **boosters**.

Aries

See **zodiac**.

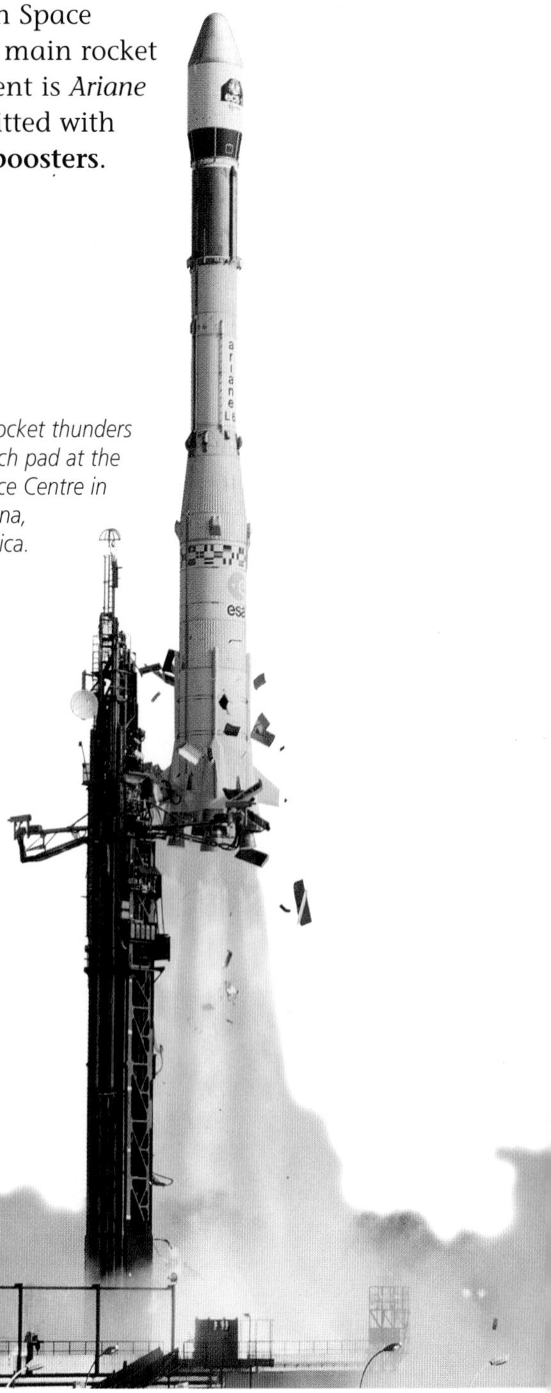

An Ariane rocket thunders off the launch pad at the Kourou Space Centre in French Guiana, South America.

Jupiter

The asteroids circle in a band, or belt, between the orbits of Mars and Jupiter.

Armstrong, Neil

See **exploring space**.

artificial satellite

See **satellite**.

asteroid

An asteroid is a small piece of rock that is found in space. It is also called a minor planet. There are many thousands of asteroids, and they are all in the **Solar System**. They were left over after the planets formed millions of years ago.
See also **asteroid belt, Ceres, planet**.

asteroid belt

The asteroid belt is a broad band in space between the planets Mars and Jupiter. Thousands of asteroids travel around the Sun in this belt.

astrolabe

An astrolabe is an instrument for measuring the position of stars. The early astronomers used astrolabes. Around the edge of the astrolabe is a scale, marked in degrees. The position of the sighting arm on the scale tells you a star's height above the horizon.

A beautiful brass astrolabe. You hold the astrolabe by the ring at the top and let it dangle. Then you sight a star by looking along the arm in the middle.

astrology

Astrology connects people's personalities and lives to the movements of the Sun, stars and planets. In astrology, every person has a star sign, which depends on the date of their birthday. The 12 star signs have the same names as the 12 constellations of the **zodiac**. Unlike **astronomy**, modern astrology is not based on scientific ideas.
See also **horoscope**.

astronaut

An astronaut is a person who travels in space. The Russian word for a space traveller is **cosmonaut**. The first American astronaut was John Glenn, who orbited the Earth in 1962.
See also **exploring space**.

NASA astronaut Loren Shriver shows one way of eating weightless chocolates on board the space shuttle Atlantis.

astronautics

Astronautics is the science and technology of space flight. The word 'astronautics' really means travelling to the stars.

astronomer

See **astronomy**.

astronomical unit (AU)

One astronomical unit equals the distance between the Earth and the Sun. It is about 150 million (150,000,000) kilometres. Astronomers use this unit to measure the huge distances in the **Solar System**.

Astronomy

When you look up at the sky on a clear night, you see thousands of stars shining down out of the velvety blackness of space. They twinkle like sparkling jewels. If you look at the night sky over a long period, you will notice that it is always changing. The silvery Moon comes and goes and changes shape. New patterns of stars come into view. Comets with long tails appear and disappear. People have been studying the night sky, or the heavens, closely for thousands of years. We call this study astronomy.

People who look at, or observe, what happens in the heavens are called astronomers. They record their observations, and they also try to explain what they see. Astronomers work in **observatories**. The main instruments that they use are telescopes. Most telescopes study the light from the stars; others study the invisible rays that stars give out, such as radio waves.

Thousands of years ago ancient astronomers like Ptolemy thought that the Earth was the centre of the Universe. They believed that the Sun, the planets and the stars all circled around the Earth.

▽

This illustration from an old astronomy book shows the planets circling round the Sun.

Then, in the 1500s, Copernicus realized that the Earth moves around the Sun, and not the other way round. In the 1600s Galileo began a revolution by observing the heavens through a telescope. Kepler worked out how the planets move.

Newton saw that a force called gravity held the Universe together. By this time astronomy had become a more exact science. In the early 1900s Einstein gave us many of our present ideas about how the Universe works.

amateur astronomer

Most astronomers are amateurs who study the heavens as a hobby. They do not work in observatories like professional astronomers. Amateur astronomers are often the first people to spot new comets and **supernovas**. When observing, they use small telescopes or binoculars, or just their eyes.

Copernicus, Nicolaus (1473–1543)

Copernicus was a priest-astronomer from Poland. He is often called the father of modern astronomy. He was the first person to realize that the Earth and all the other planets circle around the Sun.

Galileo Galilei

The Italian astronomer Galileo was the first person we know who looked at the heavens through a telescope. He made his own telescope and began observing in the winter of 1609–1610. Galileo is also known for his work on falling bodies and pendulums.

△

Galileo was the first person to spot Jupiter's large moons.

Halley, Edmond (1656–1742)

Edmond Halley was an English astronomer who was interested in comets. He worked out the **orbits** of many comets. He saw one comet in 1682 and predicted that it would return again in 1758. It did, and was called Halley's Comet.
See also **Halley's Comet.**

Herschel, William (1738–1822) and Caroline (1750–1848)

William and Caroline Herschel were born in Germany, but they became well-known astronomers in England. William discovered the planet Uranus in 1781. Caroline worked as his assistant and was also a skilled observer. She discovered six new comets.
See also **Uranus.**

Hubble, Edwin (1889–1953)

Edwin Hubble was an American astronomer. In the 1920s, he discovered that there are other galaxies outside our own star system. He also found that all the galaxies are rushing away from us.
See also **red shift.**

The American astronomer Edwin Hubble at work in 1923 in the Mount Wilson Observatory, California, USA.

Invisible astronomy

Invisible astronomy studies the invisible rays that the stars give out. These rays include gamma rays, X-rays, ultraviolet rays, infrared rays and radio waves. Astronomers uses **radio telescopes** to look at some of these waves.
See also **radiation, satellite.**

Kepler, Johannes (1571–1630)

Johannes Kepler was a German astronomer who worked out exactly how the planets travel around the Sun. He found that they travel in **orbits** that are elliptical, or oval, in shape. Before his time, astronomers thought that planets travelled in circles.

Newton, Isaac (1642–1727)

The English scientist Isaac Newton was the first to realize what holds the Solar System together. It is a force called **gravity**. The story goes that he worked out his ideas about gravity after seeing apples fall off a tree. Newton also built the first reflecting telescope.

Ptolemy

Ptolemy was an ancient Greek astronomer who lived in Alexandria around AD 150. He wrote a book that contained the knowledge and ideas held by the astronomers of his time. It was called *Almagest* (The Greatest). It included the idea that the Earth was the centre of the Universe, with all the other heavenly objects circling round it.

Space astronomy

Space astronomy involves studying the heavens from space. It uses telescopes and other instruments that are sent into space on satellites and probes. Up in space, these instruments are above the Earth's **atmosphere** and can view the stars and planets much more clearly.

This picture of a distant star cluster was taken by a space satellite named ROSAT. The satellite used the invisible X-rays given out by the cluster to take the picture.

astrophotography

Astrophotography means taking photographs of the stars. Professional astronomers usually photograph the night sky when they are observing. This is because photographic film can store light from stars that you cannot even see. It turns the faint light from very distant stars into pictures.

Atlantis

See **orbiter**.

atmosphere

An atmosphere is a layer of gases around a planet, a moon or a star. The Earth has an atmosphere that is made up of air. The atmosphere of Venus is mainly carbon dioxide gas. Most small bodies in space, including our Moon, have no atmosphere.

atom

An atom is the smallest piece of any material that can exist. All matter is made up of atoms. Different kinds of matter are made up of different kinds of atoms. In nature, there are 92 different kinds of atom.
See also **element**, **molecule**.

The Earth's atmosphere seen from space. It contains layers of dust from an erupting volcano.

aurora

An aurora is a colourful glow in the night sky. It appears in far northern and far southern parts of the Earth. In the north it is often called the northern lights, and in the south the southern lights. An aurora can sometimes look like a shimmering curtain of coloured lights.
See also **flare**.

△
The aurora borealis, or northern lights, brightens the night sky in the far north of the Earth.

▽
The Earth's axis passes through the centre of the Earth and the North and South Poles.

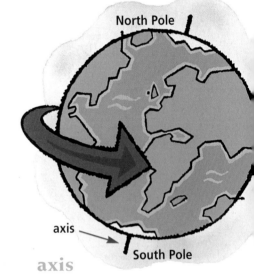

North Pole

axis

South Pole

▽
Every atom has a centre part, or nucleus. Tiny electrons circle around the nucleus.

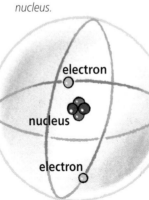

electron

nucleus

electron

axis

An axis is a line around which an object can spin. The Earth's axis is an imaginary line that passes through the centre of the Earth. The Earth rotates (spins round) in space on its axis. Other planets, as well as the Sun and moons, spin round an axis in the same way.

Baikonur Cosmodrome

See **spaceport**.

Beehive

The Beehive is a group of stars in the constellation Cancer. You can see it with the naked eye. It is an example of an open **cluster** of stars.

Beta Centauri

See **Alpha Centauri**, **star**.

Betelgeuse

Betelgeuse is one of the biggest stars that we know about. It is a supergiant star in the constellation Orion, and measures over 400 kilometres across. See also **Orion, star**.

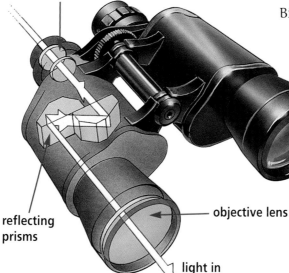

In binoculars, the light entering the front lens is reflected by glass prisms into the eyepiece.

eyepiece lens

reflecting prisms

objective lens

light in

Big Dipper

See **Plough**.

binary star

See **double star**.

binoculars

Binoculars are a kind of telescope. You use them to study the stars at night. Unlike a telescope, a pair of binoculars has two tubes, one for each eye. Binoculars are handy for star-gazing because they collect more light than your eyes, and so they make the sky look brighter. See also **telescope**.

The Big Bang created our Universe. At first, the Universe was very hot and full of radiation (rays). Matter did not form until later.

Big Bang

Most astronomers now believe that the Universe was born in a kind of explosion. They call it the Big Bang. It happened about 15,000 million years ago. At first the Universe was very tiny, but then it began to expand (get bigger) all the time. Astronomers say that the Universe is still expanding today.

Big Crunch

Some astronomers think that the Universe will end in a Big Crunch. This is the opposite of the **Big Bang**. With the Big Bang, the Universe started to get bigger. Astronomers think that one day the Universe will start to shrink (get smaller). Finally, it will shrink to such a small size that everything in it will be crunched together.

C

black hole

A black hole is an area in space that
has very strong pulling
forces. The pull of its
gravity is so
great that the
black hole
swallows
anything
near it. Not
even light
can escape from a
black hole, which is why it
is black. Black holes form
when very large stars die.
See also **star**.

◁ When matter
falls into a
black hole, it
disappears
and is never
seen again.

booster

A booster is a kind of rocket. It
is fitted to a launch vehicle and gives
extra power at lift-off. When a
booster runs out of fuel, it falls
away from the vehicle.
See also **rocket**,
space shuttle.

brightness

See **magnitude**.

brown dwarf

A brown dwarf is
a small object
that is made up
of gas and dust.
It is like a very
dim star. It will
never shine
brightly like a
proper star.

▷ Each of the two
booster rockets
that help launch
the space shuttle
parachutes back
to Earth. The
boosters can then
be used again.

Buran

Buran is the name of the Russian space shuttle.
It flew only once, in November 1988. It had no
crew on board.

▽
*Callisto, the second
biggest moon of
Jupiter, is nearly the
same size as the planet
Mercury. It is made up
of rock and ice.*

Callisto

Callisto is one of Jupiter's four big moons. It is
the third largest moon in the Solar System, and
measures 4820 kilometres across.
See also **Jupiter**.

canal (on Mars)

In the 19th century, an Italian astronomer
named Giovanni Schiaparelli claimed he had
seen canals (waterways) on the planet Mars.
Some people began to believe that there must
be intelligent creatures living on the planet
who built the canals. Space probes have
shown us that there are no canals on Mars,
and so there is no proof of intelligent life on
the planet.

Cancer

See **zodiac**.

Canopus

See **star**.

Cape Canaveral

Cape Canaveral is the main launch site for American spacecraft. It is situated on the east coast of Florida, in the USA. It has been in use since the beginning of the Space Age. The famous Kennedy Space Center is located a few kilometres inland from Cape Canaveral.
See also **Kennedy Space Center**.

Capella

See **star**.

Capricornus

See **zodiac**.

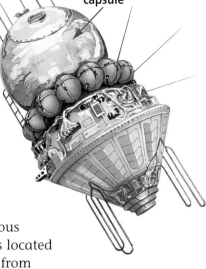

capsule

△

The first man in space, Yuri Gagarin, travelled in the round capsule of this spacecraft, called Vostok 1.

capsule

A capsule is a very small cabin inside some spacecraft. The first astronauts rode into space in a small cramped capsule.
See also **Gemini spacecraft**, **Mercury spacecraft**.

celestial

Celestial means to do with the heavens. It describes the sky and space all around the Earth.

celestial sphere

Ancient astronomers believed that the heavens formed a great dark ball around the Earth. They called this ball the celestial sphere. They thought that the stars were fixed to the inside of the sphere. We now know that there is no celestial sphere, but astronomers use the idea to find the position of stars.

centrifuge

A centrifuge is a machine that astronauts use when they are training for space. They sit inside a cabin, called a gondola, and are whirled around at high speed. This movement creates the same kind of forces that the astronauts will experience when they are blasted off into space.
See also **g-force**.

Ceres

Ceres is a big ball of rock in space. It is the largest **asteroid**. It measures about 1000 kilometres across. An Italian astronomer named Giuseppe Piazzi discovered Ceres on 1 January 1801.

Challenger

See **orbiter**.

◁ *Russian cosmonauts train inside this centrifuge. They sit in the cabin at the end of the long arm.*

Charon

Charon is the only moon of the tiny planet Pluto. It is half the size of Pluto, and measures about 1200 kilometres across.

In this photograph you can see Charon (on the right) with its parent planet, Pluto.

chemical element

See **element**.

chromosphere

The chromosphere is a pinkish layer of gases above the bright surface of the Sun. You can only see it during a total **eclipse** of the Sun, when the Sun's surface is covered.

Clavius

Clavius is a crater on the surface of the Moon. It is the largest crater that we can easily see. Clavius is situated near the Moon's south pole, and measures over 230 kilometres across.

cluster

A cluster is a group of stars that travel together in space. If the stars are loose, it is called an open cluster. If they are bunched up, it is a **globular cluster**. Galaxies also collect together to form clusters. Our own galaxy, called the Milky Way, belongs to a cluster called the Local Group.
See also **Beehive, Hyades, Pleiades**.

Coal Sack

The Coal Sack is a dark area in the night sky. It lies in the constellation Crux, or Southern Cross. It is a dark **nebula**.
See also **Crux**.

collapsar

A collapsar is a star that has collapsed. When stars die, they collapse and become much tinier than their original size. Collapsars become very dense (heavy) for their size.
See also **black hole, neutron star, white dwarf**.

Columbia

See **orbiter**.

comet

A comet is a lump of ice and dust that moves around the Sun. Comets usually measure only about 10–20 kilometres across.

For most of the time a comet stays frozen solid, and you cannot see it. When it moves closer to the Sun, it starts to melt. Some of the ice turns to gas, and a lot of dust escapes. Together they form a huge cloud that reflects sunlight well. Then you can see the comet as a great shining ball, often with a long tail.
See also **Giotto probe, Hale–Bopp, Halley's Comet, Solar System**.

Comets often grow a long tail when they approach the Sun. The tail always points away from the Sun.

This is part of a comet called Shoemaker–Levy 9. The comet broke up into pieces, which crashed into Jupiter in 1994.

communications satellite

See **satellite**.

constellation

A constellation is a pattern of bright stars in the night sky. The stars may look quite close together because they appear in the same part of the sky. In fact they are really very far apart.

Astronomers recognize 88 different constellations. Ancient astronomers named most of them over 2000 years ago. They named the constellations after animals, people and objects that looked like the patterns of stars, for example a lion, a swan and a scorpion. All these animals, people and objects appeared in traditional stories, or myths.

Modern astronomers still use the same names that the ancient astronomers gave to the constellations. The names are usually in Latin, with the English translation. Examples of constellations are Leo (the Lion), Cygnus (the Swan) and Scorpius (the Scorpion).
See also **star**, **zodiac**.

△ This beautiful star map shows Leo, the Lion, one of the signs of the zodiac.

▽ Three constellations that appear in the northern night sky. Ursa Major includes the well-known star pattern, the Plough.

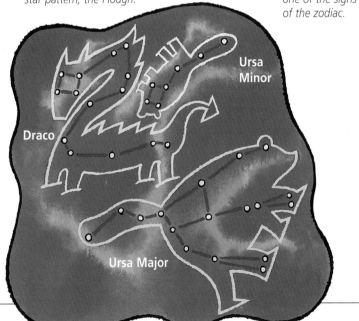

Draco

Ursa Minor

Ursa Major

Copernicus

Copernicus is the name of a large crater on the Moon. It is found in an area called the Ocean of Storms. It stands out brilliantly at the time of the Full Moon, when it is surrounded by bright **crater rays**.
See also **Moon**.

Copernicus, Nicolaus

See **astronomy**.

This photograph shows the corona spreading out into space during a total eclipse of the Sun.

corona

The corona is a faint ring of gases around the Sun. The word 'corona' means crown. From Earth, you can only see the corona during a total **eclipse** of the Sun. It appears as a pearly white halo around the dark circle of the Moon.

cosmic ray

Cosmic rays are moving through outer space towards the Earth. They are narrow beams of **radiation**. The rays would be harmful to living things if they reached the ground. Fortunately, most of the rays are blocked by the Earth's atmosphere.

cosmology

Cosmology is the study of how the Universe began. It also looks at how the Universe has changed since its beginning. Cosmologists (astronomers who study cosmology) also try to work out what might happen to the Universe in the future.
See also **Big Bang**, **Big Crunch**.

cosmonaut

Cosmonaut is the Russian name for people who travel in space. Yuri Gagarin became the first cosmonaut, and the first person in space, when he flew into space on 12 April 1961.
See also **astronaut**.

The Russian cosmonaut Valentina Tereshkova was the first woman in space. She piloted the Vostok 6 spacecraft for three days in June 1963.

cosmos

Cosmos is another word for the Universe.

countdown

A countdown is the time before a launch vehicle lifts off into space. The time is counted backwards from the time of the lift-off, which is known as T. So T minus 3 hours in a countdown means that there are 3 hours left before lift-off.

Crab Nebula

The Crab Nebula is a huge cloud of gas that looks a bit like a crab. It is found in the constellation Taurus. It is the remains of a star that blew itself apart in the year 1054. We know this date is accurate because Chinese astronomers recorded the event.
See also **supernova**.

crater

A crater is a pit in the surface of a planet or a moon. Most craters are made when a meteorite hits the surface. But some are formed when volcanoes erupt. The Moon is covered with meteorite craters, many of them more than 100 kilometres across. Only a few meteorite craters can still be found on Earth, such as the Arizona meteor crater in the Arizona Desert, USA.

▷ *The Arizona meteor crater is the finest meteorite crater on Earth. It was formed when a huge meteorite crashed to Earth about 50,000 years ago. The crater measures 1265 metres across and is 175 metres deep.*

crater ray

Crater rays are streaks of bright material. They can be seen coming from large craters on the Moon. They show up best at the time of the Full Moon.

▽ *The Crab Nebula is the remains of a huge star that exploded more than 900 years ago*

Crescent Moon

See **phases of the Moon**.

crust

The crust is the hard outer layer of a planet or a moon. The Earth's crust is made up of rock, but the crust of some moons is made up mainly of ice.

▽ *Crux, the Southern Cross, can only be seen by observers in the southern half of the world.*

Crux

Crux is the best-known constellation in the southern hemisphere. It is also called the Southern Cross. It lies close to two of the brightest stars in the sky, Alpha Centauri and Beta Centauri.

D

dark matter

Dark matter is material in the Universe that you cannot see. It is invisible because it does not give off light or reflect the light from stars.

day

Day is the time when the place where you live receives light from the Sun. Day begins when the Sun rises above the **horizon** in the morning. It ends when the Sun sets below the horizon in the evening.

Day and night are caused by the Earth spinning round. It is day when a place spins into the sunlight.

Sun

Earth spins round

day

night

The day is also a basic unit of time. It is equal to 24 hours. It is the amount of time that the Earth takes to spin all the way round once on its **axis**.
See also **night**, **time**.

Deep Space Network

The Deep Space Network keeps track of spacecraft up in space. It is a system of tracking stations. NASA uses it to track and communicate with distant space probes. The tracking stations use huge dish aerials that measure up to 70 metres across. Sometimes they also use **radio telescopes**.

This giant dish aerial, at Goldstone, California, USA, is part of the Deep Space Network.

Delta rocket

The Delta rocket is used to launch satellites into space. It is one of the USA's most reliable **launch vehicles**. Delta rockets have successfully launched hundreds of satellites.

A Delta rocket lifts off the launch pad. Look for the cluster of booster rockets around its base.

Deneb

See **star**.

Discovery

See **orbiter**.

docking

Docking is what happens when two spacecraft join together in space.

Dog Star

See **Sirius**.

E

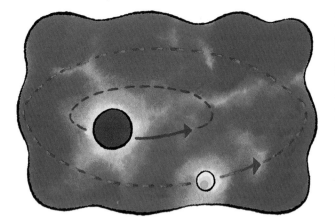

We call this kind of double-star system a binary star. In a binary star, two stars circle around each other and it is often difficult to tell them apart.

double star

A double star is a pair of stars that seem to be close together in the sky. Some stars look like doubles because they happen to be in the same part of the sky. In other double stars, the two stars are really close together and circle around one another. We call this kind of double star a binary star.
See also **Algol**.

drag

Drag is a force that pushes against objects when they travel through the air. Another term for drag is air resistance. Spacecraft use drag as a brake when they return to Earth. It slows them down so that they can land safely.
See also **re-entry**.

dwarf star

A dwarf star is a small star. It is a lot smaller than a giant star or a supergiant star. Our own Sun is a yellow dwarf star, even though it measures nearly 1,400,000 kilometres across.
See also **brown dwarf, white dwarf**.

Earth ⊕

We live on the planet Earth. It is the only planet in the **Solar System** where we know that there are living things. The Earth is a ball of rock that measures 12,756 kilometres across the middle. It has two main surface features: land and sea. The Earth is surrounded by a layer of gases that we call the **atmosphere**. It has one natural satellite, the Moon.
See also **Moon, planet**.

earthgrazer

An earthgrazer is an object in space that passes quite close to the Earth. It is a kind of **asteroid**. It is also called a near-earth object (NEO).

Earth-resources satellite

See **satellite**.

A view of the Earth seen from space. The main land areas that you can see are Africa and the Arabian Peninsula.

earthshine

Near the time of the New Moon, the dark part of the Moon sometimes shines faintly. We call this earthshine, because the Moon is reflecting light coming from the Earth.
See also **phases of the Moon**.

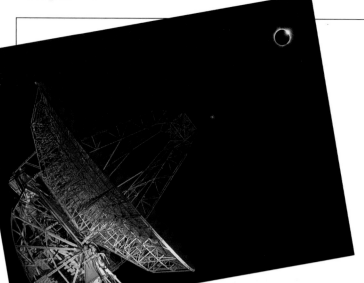

A total eclipse of the Sun, seen at a space tracking station. This stage of the eclipse is known as the 'diamond ring'.

eclipse

An eclipse happens when an object in space moves in front of another and blots out its light. Sometimes the Moon, as seen from Earth, moves in front of the Sun and cuts off its light. The Earth enters the Moon's shadow. We call this an eclipse of the Sun, or a solar eclipse. Sometimes the Earth moves between the Sun and the Moon. The Moon passes into the Earth's shadow. We call this an eclipse of the Moon, or a lunar eclipse.

Solar eclipses usually take place two or three times a year. They can only be seen in certain places and over a small area. When only part of the Sun is covered up, we call this a partial eclipse.

When the whole Sun is covered, it is a total eclipse. A total eclipse only lasts for a few minutes. Daylight suddenly turns into night. Solar eclipses are so exciting to watch that many people travel a long way to have the best view of them.
See also **chromosphere, corona**.

Einstein, Albert

See **relativity**.

element

An element is a basic building block that makes up all materials. Every different kind of material, or matter – metals, plastics, plants or blood – is made up of one or more elements. In the world around us we can find about 90 different elements. As far as we know, these same elements are found throughout the Universe.
See also **atom, molecule**.

elliptical

Something that is elliptical has an oval shape. It is the shape of an ellipse. The planets travel around the Sun in elliptical **orbits**. Many galaxies are elliptical in shape.

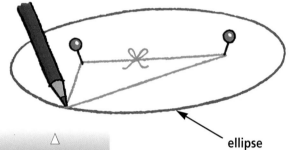

ellipse

To draw an ellipse, first loop a piece of string between two pins. Put a pencil in the loop and move it round the pins.

On Earth, the Equator passes through the continents of South America and Africa.

encounter

An encounter is a meeting. A space probe makes a planetary encounter when it arrives at its target planet.

Endeavour

See **orbiter**.

equator

An equator is an imaginary line around the middle of a planet. It is a line halfway between the planet's poles. It divides the planet into two halves, called hemispheres. They are the northern hemisphere and the southern hemisphere.
See also **axis**.

North Pole

Equator

South Pole

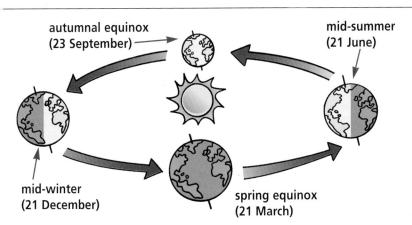

autumnal equinox
(23 September)

mid-summer
(21 June)

mid-winter
(21 December)

spring equinox
(21 March)

The Earth is tilted as it travels round the Sun. After the spring equinox, the northern half of the world is tilted towards the Sun and the days grow longer. After the autumnal equinox, the northern half is tilted away from the Sun and the days grow shorter.

equinox

An equinox is a time when days and nights last the same length of time all over the world. The name 'equinox' means equal nights. There are two equinoxes each year. The spring equinox falls on or near 21 March, and the autumnal equinox falls on or near 23 September.

ESA

See **European Space Agency**.

escape velocity

Escape velocity is the speed that a spacecraft has to reach in order to leave the Earth and travel to the Moon or the planets. It is the speed needed to escape from Earth's **gravity**. The Earth's escape velocity is about 40,000 kilometres an hour, which is more than ten times the speed of the fastest jet plane.
See also **probe**.

ET

See **extraterrestrial**.

European Space Agency (ESA)

The European Space Agency organizes space activities in Europe. Thirteen countries belong to the agency: Austria, Belgium, Britain, Denmark, Finland, France, Germany, Ireland, the Netherlands, Norway, Spain, Sweden and Switzerland.

EVA

See **extravehicular activity**.

evening star

An evening star shines brightly in the sky just after the Sun sets. It appears low down in the sky in the west. It is not a star but a planet, usually Venus.

Explorer 1

Explorer 1 was the first satellite launched into space by the USA. It was put into orbit on 31 January 1958. It made the first discovery of the Space Age by finding 'belts' of very strong **radiation** around the Earth.
See also **Van Allen belts**.

The ESA's astronaut Thomas Reiter (right), from Germany, is seen working in the Russian space station Mir with cosmonaut Sergei Avdeev.

Exploring space

On 4 October 1957, Russian scientists launched a rocket from central Asia. Within minutes, it had climbed above the Earth's atmosphere into space. A tiny section broke away from the rocket and began to circle the Earth, sending out radio signals: 'Beep, beep, beep'. *Sputnik 1* had become the world's first spacecraft. The age of exploring space – the Space Age – had begun.

Since that time, thousands of spacecraft have been launched. Most are satellites that circle the Earth. Others are space probes that escape from Earth to visit the Moon and planets.

Human beings began exploring space in 1961, when a Russian called Yuri Gagarin flew into orbit. Until then, no-one knew if human beings could survive flights into space. In 1965, Alexei Leonov showed that astronauts could go space walking outside their craft. In 1969, Neil Armstrong took the first human step on the surface of the Moon.

Today, astronauts and cosmonauts travel regularly into space, in spacecraft such as the space shuttle. They spend months at a time on board space stations. In the 21st century astronauts and cosmonauts might travel to Mars and set up a base there.

This famous photograph of Edwin Aldrin, the second man to walk on the Moon, was taken by his fellow astronaut, Neil Armstrong.

Gagarin, Yuri (1934–1968)

Yuri Gagarin was the first human being to travel in space, on 12 April 1961. He was a Russian **cosmonaut**. He circled the Earth once in his spacecraft *Vostok 1*, which reached a height of over 300 kilometres above the Earth. See also **Vostok**.

△

Yuri Gagarin flew into space only once. His flight lasted about one and a half hours.

▷ *The launch of a Saturn V rocket from the Kennedy Space Center in Florida. This rocket launched astronauts to the Moon.*

Armstrong, Neil (born 1930)

Neil Armstrong was the first person to walk on the Moon, on 20 July 1969. He was an American **astronaut** taking part in the first ever Moon-landing mission, *Apollo 11*. As he took his first step on the Moon's surface, he said: 'That's one small step for a man, one giant leap for mankind.'

Glenn, John (born 1921)

John Glenn became the first American astronaut to fly into space, on 20 February 1962. He circled the Earth three times in his spacecraft *Friendship 7*.

Goddard, Robert (1882–1945)

Robert Goddard built the first modern type of rocket. He launched it on 16 March 1926. It used liquid **propellants**: petrol and liquid oxygen. Goddard was an American engineer and lecturer.

Leonov, Alexei (born 1934)

Alexei Leonov was the first person to walk in space, on 18 March 1965. He was a Russian **cosmonaut**. He spent about 10 minutes outside his spacecraft, *Voskhod 2*. See also **extravehicular activity**.

Spaceship

A spaceship is a spacecraft with a human crew. The earliest spaceships were tiny and were known as capsules. They included Vostok, Mercury, Gemini and Apollo spacecraft. The Soyuz spacecraft that carries Russian cosmonauts into space is not much bigger.

In the 21st century spaceships will be built to carry astronauts to other planets. One day, starships might carry people to planets that move around stars other than our Sun.

Tereshkova, Valentina (born 1937)

Valentina Tereshkova was the first woman to travel in space. She was a Russian **cosmonaut**. She flew into space on 16 June 1963 in a Vostok spacecraft and circled the Earth 48 times.

Robert Goddard at work at his launch site in Roswell, New Mexico, USA in 1940.

Tsiolkovsky, Konstantin (1857–1935)

Konstantin Tsiolkovsky was the first person to work out the basic ideas behind space flight. He was a Russian schoolteacher who is often called the 'father of astronautics'. He realized that rockets could be used for space travel. Tsiolkovsky understood that several rockets needed to be joined together to make a **launch vehicle**.

V-2

The V-2 was a German rocket built during the Second World War. It could travel a distance of about 500 kilometres. It was 13 metres long and burned alcohol and liquid oxygen **propellants**. After the War, V-2s were taken to the United States and Russia. They were the starting point for work that led to the first space rockets.
See also **rocket**.

von Braun, Wernher (1912–1977)

Wernher von Braun designed the giant *Saturn V* rocket. It launched the Apollo spacecraft to the Moon. Von Braun was born in Germany and led the team that built the V-2 rocket during the Second World War. He went to the USA in 1945 and became chief rocket designer for the US Army.
See also **Saturn V**.

extraterrestrial

Extraterrestrial means outside the Earth, or not from the Earth. In popular language, an extraterrestrial, or ET for short, is an alien being from another world.
See also **SETI**.

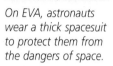

This imaginary alien is seen in front of the flying saucer that carried it to Earth.

On EVA, astronauts wear a thick spacesuit to protect them from the dangers of space.

extravehicular activity (EVA)

Extravehicular activity means everything that astronauts do in space when outside their spacecraft. The popular name for EVA is space walking.

falling star

See **meteor**.

fireball

A fireball is a very bright streak of light in the sky. It is a kind of **meteor**. It is caused by a large lump of rock that enters the Earth's **atmosphere**, and sometimes explodes.

First Quarter

See **phases of the Moon**.

flare

A flare is a great burst of light that leaps up from the surface of the Sun. It is often called a solar flare. It gives off light rays and other kinds of **radiation**, as well as very fast-moving particles (tiny pieces of matter). When these particles reach Earth, they cause **auroras** and upset radio communications.

A huge solar flare charges through the Sun's atmosphere. It is very bright, but it only lasts for a short time.

fly-by

A fly-by is a kind of space mission. During a fly-by, a spacecraft flies past a planet or another body in space. The spacecraft, which is usually a probe, does not land or go into orbit around the body.

flying saucer

See **UFO**.

Fomalhaut

See **star**.

A close-up picture of a galaxy known as M100, in the constellation Coma Berenices. There is a good view of the galaxy's spiral arms.

G

In a spacecraft, all things seem to be floating. But they are really falling, all together.

▽
Four main kinds of galaxy: spiral, irregular, barred spiral and elliptical.

free fall

Free fall describes what happens to astronauts in space. It is the proper name for **weightlessness**. When astronauts travel in space, the Earth's **gravity** is still pulling them, and they are falling. At the same time they are travelling very fast. As they fall a certain amount, the Earth below curves away from them by the same amount. In other words, they stay at the same height above the Earth.

fuel cell

A fuel cell is a kind of battery. It produces electricity from fuel gases without burning them. The space shuttle has fuel cells that use hydrogen and oxygen gases.

Full Moon

See **phases of the Moon**.

fusion

See **nuclear reaction**.

Gagarin, Yuri

See **exploring space**.

galactic

Galactic means to do with a galaxy. It usually describes our own galaxy, which we call The Galaxy.

galaxy

A galaxy is a huge island of stars in space. Stars are always found in galaxies. They are not found scattered throughout space. There are millions and millions of galaxies in the Universe. Each galaxy contains millions and millions of stars. They also contain great clouds of dust and gas called **nebulas**.

Some galaxies are shapeless and so we call them irregulars. Others have a definite shape. Galaxies shaped like a ball or an egg are called ellipticals. Galaxies that are shaped like a wheel, with curved arms, are called spirals. A spiral galaxy is a kind of flattish disc with a bulge in the middle. Most of the stars are grouped together on the arms, which curve out from the bulge. The whole galaxy spins round. From far away, it would look like a Catherine wheel firework spinning very slowly.

Some galaxies give out much more energy than ordinary galaxies. These are called active galaxies. Most of this energy comes from the centre of the galaxy. The energy from an ordinary galaxy comes mainly from its stars. Active galaxies may give off their energy as radio waves or X-rays, rather than as light rays. See also **Andromeda Galaxy**, **Magellanic Clouds**, **quasar**, **radiation**, **radio galaxy**.

spiral

irregular

barred spiral

elliptical

Galaxy, The

See **Milky Way Galaxy**.

Galileo

Galileo is a US probe that explored the planet Jupiter. On its way, it visited two **asteroids** called Gaspra and Ida. In 1995 the probe dropped a smaller probe into Jupiter's thick atmosphere. It then went into orbit around the planet.

Galileo Galilei

See **astronomy**.

gamma rays

See **radiation**.

In a geostationary orbit above the Equator, a satellite travels at the same speed as the Earth beneath it.

Ganymede

Ganymede is one of Jupiter's moons. It measures 5276 kilometres across, and is the largest moon in the **Solar System.**

geostationary orbit

35,900 km

satellite

gas giant

See **planet**.

Gemini

See **zodiac**.

The Galileo probe took this picture of Ganymede. Long ridges cover its surface, and you can also see many craters made by meteorites.

Gemini spacecraft

Gemini spacecraft carried American astronauts into space in 1965 and 1966. During the Gemini missions astronauts gained their first experience of long space flights, **docking** and space walking.
See **exploring space, extravehicular activity.**

geostationary orbit

In a geostationary orbit, a satellite stays above the same point on Earth. The orbit is nearly 36,000 kilometres above the Earth's surface. At this height, a satellite circles the Earth once every 24 hours. The Earth beneath it takes the same time to spin round once. This is why the satellite stays above the same point.

g-force

Astronauts feel g-forces tugging at their bodies when their rocket is launched into space. (The 'g' stands for **gravity**.) The rocket gives them a great push, which makes them feel very heavy. They feel as if gravity has suddenly increased.
See also **centrifuge**.

A distant view of the moon Ganymede

When Giotto flew past Halley's Comet, it was only 600 kilometres away from the comet.

Giotto

Giotto was a European space probe that flew past Halley's Comet in 1986. It sent back the first close-up pictures of a comet. It went on to visit another comet called Grigg–Skjellerup in 1992.
See also **Halley's Comet**.

Glenn, John

See **exploring space**.

This is a globular cluster in the Andromeda Galaxy. It contains about 300,000 stars.

globular cluster

A globular cluster is a large group of stars in the shape of a ball, or globe. The stars are packed together tightly. The largest globular clusters contain millions of stars. You can see some clusters with the naked eye.
See also **cluster**.

Goddard, Robert

See **exploring space**.

gravity

Gravity is the Earth's pull on everything on it and near it. It makes a stone fall to the ground when you drop it. It keeps the water in the oceans. Every other body in space has a similar pulling force. The bigger the body, the greater is the pull of its gravity.

The pull of gravity makes satellites travel in circles around Earth. You can imitate gravity by whirling a ball on a string around your head. By pulling on the string you keep the ball moving in circles.

Great Red Spot

See **Jupiter**.

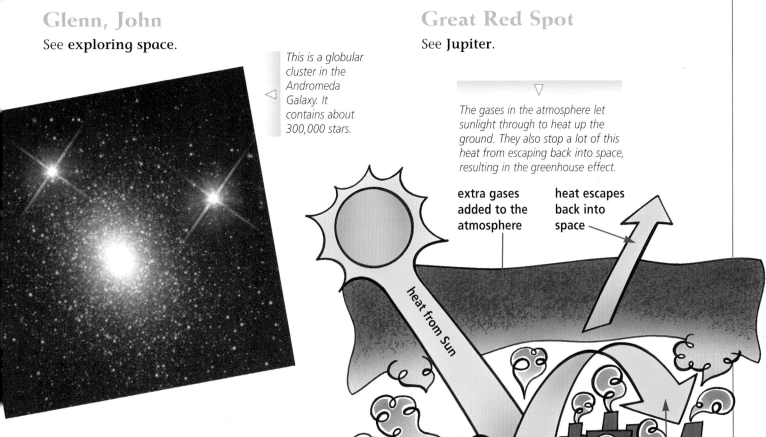

The gases in the atmosphere let sunlight through to heat up the ground. They also stop a lot of this heat from escaping back into space, resulting in the greenhouse effect.

extra gases added to the atmosphere

heat escapes back into space

heat from Sun

heat trapped by atmosphere

greenhouse effect

The greenhouse effect happens when the atmosphere around a planet traps heat and stops it escaping. The heat comes from the Sun's rays. We call it the greenhouse effect because the atmosphere traps the heat like a garden greenhouse.

Both Earth and Venus are warmed up by the greenhouse effect. On Venus, the greenhouse effect has caused the temperature on the planet's surface to rise to over 450 degrees Celsius.

Hale–Bopp

Hale–Bopp is a very bright comet. When it appeared in 1997, it was one of the brightest comets ever seen. You could easily see it with the naked eye, and it looked as bright as the brightest stars. It is named after the astronomers who discovered it in 1995, Alan Hale and Thomas Bopp.
See also **comet**.

Halley, Edmond

See **astronomy**.

Halley's Comet

Halley's Comet is the most famous comet of all. You can see it in the sky about every 75 years. The comet is named after the English astronomer Edmond Halley. He was the first person to realize that the comet regularly visits the skies above Earth.
See also **astronomy, comet**.

▷
A scene from the historic Bayeux Tapestry, showing Halley's Comet appearing before the Battle of Hastings in 1066.

heat shield

The heat shield is an outer covering on a spacecraft. It is found on spacecraft that are designed to return to Earth. When a spacecraft re-enters the Earth's atmosphere, the air rubs against it and makes it heat up. The heat shield stops the heat from damaging the spacecraft or the crew inside it.
See also **re-entry**.

heavenly body

A heavenly body is an object that appears in the night sky, or the heavens. Planets, stars and moons are all examples of heavenly bodies.

helium

Helium is an invisible gas. It is an **element**. Only small amounts of helium are found on Earth. But there is more helium in the Universe than any other substance, apart from hydrogen. When the stars make helium, they produce the energy that makes them shine.
See also **nuclear reaction**.

hemisphere

See **equator**.

Herschel, William and Caroline

See **astronomy**.

horizon

The horizon is the farthest point that you can see in any direction. It is where the sky meets the land or the sea.

horizon

△
You can see the horizon clearly at the seaside. In this picture, it is only about 4 kilometres away.

horoscope

A horoscope is a kind of chart. It is important in **astrology** because it shows the positions of the stars and planets when a person is born. Astrologers use horoscopes to tell people what might happen to them in the future.

Horsehead Nebula

The Horsehead Nebula is a dark cloud of gas in the constellation Orion. It has the shape of a horse's head.
See also **nebula**.

The Horsehead Nebula in the constellation Orion. Dark gas blocks the light from the stars behind it. ▷

Houston

People use the call sign 'Houston' when they speak to astronauts on the radio during space missions. The sign belongs to NASA's Mission Control, which is at Houston in Texas, USA.
See also **mission control**.

Hubble Space Telescope

The Hubble Space Telescope is one of the best-known space telescopes in orbit above Earth. It is a huge reflecting telescope. It has sent back to Earth the clearest images (pictures) of the Universe ever seen.
See also **astronomy**, **telescope**.

Hyades

The Hyades is a group of stars in the constellation Taurus. It is an example of an open **cluster**. You can see it with the naked eye around the reddish star Aldebaran.

hydrogen

Hydrogen is the most common substance found in the Universe. It is an **element**. The stars use hydrogen as a kind of fuel when they produce the energy that makes them shine.
See also **helium**, **nuclear reaction**.

◁ The Hubble Space Telescope, attached to the Space Shuttle Endeavour, *during repairs.*

I

ice cap

An ice cap is a covering of ice around the poles of a planet. The planets Earth and Mars have ice caps. On Earth, the ice is frozen water. On Mars, the ice is mainly frozen carbon dioxide gas, or dry ice.

infrared rays

See **radiation**.

Intelsat

Intelsat is an organization that helps to send communications around the world. It provides satellites that carry telephone, radio and television signals. The name Intelsat is short for the International Telecommunications Satellite Organization. More than 110 countries belong to Intelsat. See also **satellite**.

intergalactic

Intergalactic means between the galaxies.

interplanetary

Interplanetary means between the planets.

interstellar

Interstellar means between the stars.

interstellar matter

Interstellar matter is the material between the stars. The spaces between the stars contain a lot of hydrogen and specks of dust. Sometimes this material forms thick clouds, which we see as **nebulas**.

invisible astronomy

See **astronomy**.

The northern ice cap can be clearly seen in this photograph of the planet Mars. The ice cap melts and shrinks during the Martian summer.

A volcano erupts on the surface of Io. It has been nicknamed the 'pizza moon' because of its many colours.

Io

Io is one of the four big moons of Jupiter. It is one of the most unusual moons in the **Solar System**. It is a very bright orange colour, and there are active volcanoes on its surface.

ionosphere

The ionosphere is one of the layers of air around the Earth. It is part of the Earth's **atmosphere**. It starts about 50 kilometres above the Earth's surface, and ends about 400 kilometres up. **Auroras** take place in the ionosphere.

IRAS

See **satellite**.

J

jettison

Jettison means to push to one side or throw away. As a **launch vehicle** goes up into space, it jettisons its rocket stages, one by one.

The rockets that make up a launch vehicle are jettisoned, one by one. They fall back to the ground and break up.

Jewel Box

The Jewel Box is a group of stars in the constellation Crux. It is an example of an open **cluster**. It has this name because the stars in it are many different colours.

Jodrell Bank

Jodrell Bank is a very important centre where astronomers work. It is an **observatory** in Cheshire, in northern England. Its main instrument is a giant **radio telescope** with a dish that measures 76 metres across.

nose cone

2nd stage

1st stage

booster

Jovian

Jovian means to do with the planet Jupiter. The Jovian moons are the moons of Jupiter.

Jupiter

Jupiter is by far the biggest planet in the Solar System. It measures more than 142,000 kilometres across, which is 11 times bigger than Earth. Jupiter is made up mainly of the gases hydrogen and helium. Underneath Jupiter's **atmosphere**, the hydrogen has turned into a cold liquid. On many nights you can see Jupiter shining in the sky like a very bright star. See also **planet, Solar System**.

The colourful atmosphere of Jupiter is marked by many dark and light bands, called belts and zones. They are really fast-moving clouds.

The biggest spot in Jupiter's atmosphere is the Great Red Spot (right). It is a huge storm centre measuring about 40,000 kilometres wide.

Kennedy Space Center

The Kennedy Space Center is one of the busiest spaceports in the world. It is in Florida, in the USA. The space shuttle takes off and lands there. The Center is named after the US President John F. Kennedy, who started the project to land Apollo spacecraft on the Moon.
See also **Cape Canaveral**, **exploring space**.

Space dog Laika in her spacecraft just before her flight. The Russians often used dogs on test flights into space.

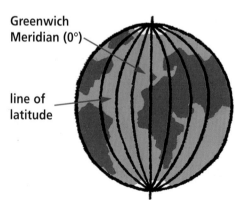

△

The 'rocket park' at the Kennedy Space Center. Rockets like these carried the first American astronauts into space.

Kepler, Johannes

See **astronomy**.

Kourou Space Centre

The Kourou Space Centre is the main launching site for the European Space Agency. It is in French Guiana, on the Atlantic coast of South America. All the Ariane rockets are launched from there.
See also **Ariane**, **European Space Agency**.

Laika

The dog Laika was the very first space traveller.
She was launched into space on board the satellite *Sputnik 2* in November 1957. The satellite did not return to Earth.

Landsat

See **satellite**.

Large Magellanic Cloud

See **Magellanic Clouds**.

Last Quarter

See **phases of the Moon**.

▽

On Earth, latitude tells you how far a place is north or south of the Equator. Longitude tells you how far the place is east or west from the Greenwich Meridian, the line of longitude that passes through Greenwich, England.

line of longitude

Equator (0°) →

Greenwich Meridian (0°)

line of latitude

latitude and longitude

You can find where a place is on Earth from its latitude and longitude. Astronomers use latitude and longitude to describe where places are on other planets, and to give the position of stars in the **celestial sphere**. Latitude and longitude are measured in degrees (°).

launch vehicle

A launch vehicle carries spacecraft into space. It is made up of several rockets that are joined together. The rockets fire in turn, one after the other. This arrangement is called a step rocket. The space shuttle is the main launch vehicle for US astronauts. The Ariane and Delta rockets are important launch vehicles for satellites.
See also **Ariane, Delta rocket, lift-off.**

fuel tank

orbiter

booster

main engine

The space shuttle is a launch vehicle with two sets of rockets – boosters and main engines.

Leonov, Alexei

See **exploring space.**

Libra

See **zodiac.**

life in space

The Earth is the only place where we know there is life. It has millions and millions of different living things. They range from tiny creatures that you can see only through a microscope, to huge whales that are bigger than houses. Scientists have found some chemicals in space that are the building blocks of life. So it is possible that there may be life somewhere among the stars.
See also **alien, SETI.**

life-support system

A life-support system keeps astronauts alive in space. All spacecraft that carry people need to have one. The system supplies the crew's cabin with air. It also keeps the cabin at a comfortable temperature and removes stale air and smells.

launch window

A launch window is the right time to launch a spacecraft into space. Every spacecraft has to be launched into the right path in space. To reach this path, it must be launched during a certain period of time – the launch window.

With all its engines blazing, the space shuttle Discovery lifts off the launch pad at the Kennedy Space Center in Florida.

Leo

See **zodiac.**

lift-off

Lift-off is the moment when a launch vehicle leaves the ground and heads towards space.

light

We need light in order to see things. Most light in our world comes from the Sun. Light rays are one kind of **radiation** that the Sun gives out. It also gives out invisible rays, including heat rays. All the other stars give out light and invisible rays too.

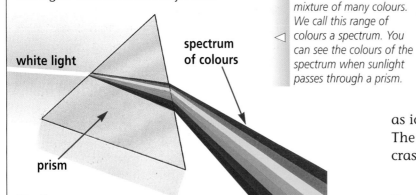

White sunlight is a mixture of many colours. We call this range of colours a spectrum. You can see the colours of the spectrum when sunlight passes through a prism.

white light

spectrum of colours

prism

light-year

A light-year is the distance that a beam of light travels in one year. Astronomers measure distances in space in light-years. One light-year equals nearly 10 million million kilometres. The nearest stars to Earth are more than 4 light-years away.
See also **astronomy**, **parsec**.

Local Group

The Local Group is a small group of galaxies. Our Milky Way Galaxy belongs to this group, or **cluster**, of galaxies. The Andromeda Galaxy and the Magellanic Clouds are also part of the Local Group.

longitude

See **latitude and longitude**.

Luna probes

Luna probes were sent to the Moon by the Russians. *Luna 2* was the very first probe to hit the Moon, in 1959. Other Luna probes landed on the Moon and went into orbit around it. *Luna 17* landed the robot explorer *Lunokhod*.
See also **Lunokhod**, **probe**.

lunar

Lunar means to do with the Moon. Lunar craters are craters on the surface of the Moon.

lunar eclipse

See **eclipse**.

Lunar Prospector

The US space probe *Lunar Prospector* went to the Moon in 1998 to look for water. It found water that had frozen as ice near the Moon's north and south poles. The water probably came from **comets** that crashed on the Moon long ago.

Lunar Rover

See **Moon buggy**.

The Large Magellanic Cloud is the closest galaxy to our own galaxy, the Milky Way.

Lunokhod

Lunokhod was the first wheeled vehicle to travel on the Moon. The Russians sent it to the Moon in 1970. They steered it from Earth using radio waves.

The Russian space vehicle Lunokhod (the word means 'moonwalker'). It had two TV cameras as 'eyes', and its wheels were driven by electric motors.

M

M number

Astronomers use M numbers to describe objects in space. M1 is the Crab Nebula; M31 is the Andromeda Galaxy. M numbers belong to a list of **nebulas** and galaxies that was drawn up by a French astronomer called Charles Messier in 1781.

Magellan

Magellan was a US space probe that visited Venus in 1989. The probe went into orbit around the planet, and used **radar** to look at the surface. Ordinary photographs cannot show the surface because it is covered with thick cloud.

Magellanic Clouds

The Large and the Small Magellanic Clouds are two nearby galaxies. You can see them as misty patches in the night sky in far southern parts of the world.

magnitude

The magnitude of a star tells you how bright it is. The brightest stars you can see are stars of the first magnitude. The dimmest stars you can see are stars of the sixth magnitude. See also **star**.

manned manoeuvring unit (MMU)

A manned manoeuvring unit is a backpack that astronauts sometimes wear outside their spacecraft. It helps them to move about in space. Astronauts fire jets of gas from the unit in order to move around.

mare, maria

See **sea (on the Moon)**.

Mariner

Mariner is the name of several US probes that explored different planets. *Mariner 4* was the first probe to send back pictures of a planet, Mars, in 1965. *Mariner 10* took the first and only close-up pictures of Mercury in 1973. See also **probe**.

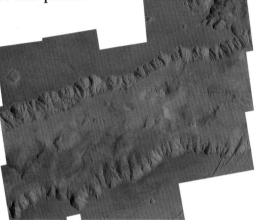

△

Mariner Valley, on the surface of Mars, is about 5000 kilometres long. It is named after the Mariner probe that discovered it.

Mariner Valley

Mariner Valley is a huge series of valleys on the planet Mars. It is the biggest valley system that we know in the **Solar System**. It is much bigger than the famous Grand Canyon in the USA.

life-support system

spacesuit control and display panel

hand controller

MMU

spacesuit

An astronaut 'flies' in space with an MMU. He uses the hand controllers to fire gas from the 24 little jets that are dotted around the unit.

Mars

Mars is one of the nearest planets to Earth. Sometimes you can see it shining brightly in the sky. It is easy to spot because it is reddish in colour. That is why we call it the Red Planet.

Mars is a rocky planet like Earth, but it is much smaller. It is only about half as big across as Earth. People once used to think there were intelligent beings on Mars, but there are not.
See also **canal (on Mars)**, **planet**, **Solar System**.

Martian

Martian means to do with Mars. A Martian crater is a crater on the surface of Mars.

△
The surface of Mars, photographed by the Pathfinder probe which landed on the planet in 1997.

mass

The mass of an object means the amount of material it contains. We call objects massive when they contain a lot of material, or matter. Stars, for example, are massive.

Mass is not the same as weight. The weight of an object is the force of **gravity** that pulls on the object. If the gravity changes, then so does the object's weight. But its mass stays the same.

matter

The Universe is made up of two main things – matter and empty space. Matter can have three different forms. It can be a gas, such as air. It can be a liquid, such as water. Or it can be a solid, such as rock. All matter is made up of **atoms** and **elements**.

Mercury

Mercury is the closest planet to the Sun. This explains why it is a very hot planet. Mercury is rocky like Earth, but it is much smaller. It is only about one-third as big across as Earth. Mercury is covered in craters and looks like the Moon.
See also **planet**, **Solar System**.

Mercury spacecraft

Mercury spacecraft carried the first US astronauts into space. The crew cabin, or capsule, was about the same size as a telephone box.
See also **exploring space**.

△
A close-up view of the cratered surface of Mercury. Temperatures on the planet reach up to 480 degrees Celsius.

▷ *A flaming meteor plunges to Earth. It is a piece of rock that heats up as it rubs against the air. The rock becomes so hot that it catches fire.*

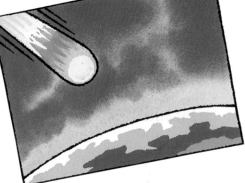

meteor

A meteor is a streak of light that you can see in the night sky. It is also called a shooting star or a falling star. The streak appears when a piece of rock from space enters the Earth's **atmosphere** and burns up.
See also **meteor shower**.

meteorite

A meteorite is a lump of rock or metal from space. Meteorites fall through the atmosphere and land on Earth.
See also **crater**.

◁ *This meteorite fell to Earth thousands of years ago. Scientists think that it may have come from Mars.*

meteoroid

A meteoroid is a tiny speck of rock or metal found in space. When meteoroids fall through the Earth's **atmosphere**, they cause **meteors**.

meteor shower

At certain times of the year you can see many more streaks of light than usual in the night sky. This is because there is a shower of **meteors**. Heavy meteor showers often take place in late July and in mid-November.

Meteosat

See **satellite**.

Milky Way

The Milky Way is a misty band of light in the night sky. On a clear night you can often see it arching across the sky. It is the view you get of the **Milky Way Galaxy** from inside it. With binoculars or a telescope, you can see that the Milky Way is made up of thousands of stars packed closely together.

Milky Way Galaxy

The Milky Way Galaxy is the galaxy to which we belong – it is our own galaxy. Sometimes we just call it The Galaxy. The Sun and all the stars you see in the sky belong to it. Astronomers believe that altogether the Milky Way Galaxy contains 100,000 million stars. It is a spiral galaxy.
See also **galaxy**, **Milky Way**.

Mimosa

See **star**.

minor planet

See **asteroid**.

▽

Thousands of stars and shining clouds of gas make up the Milky Way. This picture shows one of the brightest parts of the Milky Way. It lies in the constellation Sagittarius.

Mir

Mir is a Russian space station that was launched in 1986. Cosmonauts have lived on it since that time. Some have stayed in space for a year or more. American astronauts visited *Mir* for the first time in 1995. Cosmonauts rode up to the space station in Soyuz spacecraft. American astronauts travelled to it in the space shuttle.
See also **Soyuz**.

Miranda

Miranda is one of Saturn's moons. It has a very strange surface. It looks as if it was once smashed to pieces and then the pieces joined together again.

core module

Soyuz ferry

△
The Russian space station Mir *was built in stages by adding new modules (parts) to the core module.*

◁ *Miranda has a patchwork surface, showing many different kinds of features.*

mission

A space mission is a journey into space.

mission control

Mission control is the control centre for a space mission. The control centre for NASA's space shuttle missions is at Houston, Texas. The Houston Mission Control is in charge of all space shuttle flights after they have been launched. Russia's main mission control centre is at Kaliningrad, outside Moscow.

MMU

See **manned manoeuvring unit**.

module

A module is a part, or unit, of an object. The large units that make up a spacecraft are often called modules. The Apollo spacecraft, for example, were made up of three modules.

▽
NASA's Mission Control at Houston, where the flight controllers sit in front of rows of computers. A controller called CapCom talks to the astronauts in space.

molecule

All materials are made up of atoms. Usually, they are linked together in groups called molecules. Astronomers have found many molecules in outer space, including water.
See also **atom**.

Moon

The Moon is Earth's closest neighbour in space. It lies on average about 384,000 kilometres away. The Moon is Earth's only natural **satellite**. It is much smaller than Earth and measures only 3476 kilometres across. It is about the same width as the USA.

The Moon is a rocky body. Its surface is made up of light-coloured highlands and dark-coloured plains. We call the plains *maria,* which means seas. Ancient astronomers thought they were great oceans, but there is no water in them. The Moon's surface is covered with **craters**. Some are small but many are over 100 kilometres across.

The Moon does not give out any light of its own. It shines because it reflects light from the Sun. From Earth we only ever see one side of the Moon. This happens because of the way the Moon spins round slowly as it circles the Earth. It takes about a month to travel all the way round the Earth.

The Moon has only a low gravity (a weak pull) because it is a small body. On the Moon you could probably do a high jump of 4 metres or more! The low gravity means that the Moon cannot hold onto any air, or atmosphere. So astronauts who explore the Moon must wear spacesuits in order to breathe air.
See also **Clavius, phases of the Moon, sea (on the Moon), tide.**

Once a month we see a Full Moon, when the whole nearside of the Moon is lit up by the Sun. Then we can see that most of this side is covered by the darker-coloured maria, or seas.

moon

A moon travels around a planet. It is a natural **satellite** of a planet. Most planets in the Solar System have moons. Earth has one, called the Moon. The planets Jupiter and Saturn have at least 39 moons altogether.

Moon buggy

Moon buggy is the popular name for a small vehicle that travels on the Moon. Its proper name is the Lunar Rover, or lunar roving vehicle. The Apollo astronauts used a Moon buggy to carry themselves and their equipment when they explored the surface of the Moon. See also **Apollo spacecraft, exploring space.**

Moon probe

A Moon probe is a spacecraft, without a crew, that visits the Moon.
See also **Luna probes, Lunar Prospector, Lunokhod, Ranger, Surveyor.**

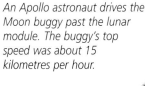

An Apollo astronaut drives the Moon buggy past the lunar module. The buggy's top speed was about 15 kilometres per hour.

morning star

A morning star shines brightly in the morning sky. It shines low in the eastern sky just before the Sun rises. It is not really a star but a planet, usually Venus.

N

naked eye

To see with the naked eye means to look at something just with your eyes. You do not use binoculars or a telescope when you see with the naked eye.

▷ The NASA emblem, or logo, is commonly called the 'meatball'. All American astronauts wear the embroidered logo on their flight suits.

NASA

NASA stands for the National Aeronautics and Space Administration. It is the organization that deals with space activities in the USA. NASA was started on 1 October 1958.

nebula

A nebula is a cloud of gas and dust. Nebulas are found in the spaces between the stars. Some nebulas are bright. They give off their own light or reflect the light from nearby stars. Others are dark, and you only see them when they blot out the light from stars behind them. See also **Crab Nebula**, **Orion Nebula**, **planetary nebula**.

◁ The columns of dark gas in the Eagle Nebula are known as 'pillars of creation'. This is because stars are forming in them.

Neptune ♆

Neptune is a large and faraway planet. It measures about four times bigger across than Earth. It is so far away that you can only see it through a telescope. It is made up mainly of gas, like Jupiter. See also **astronomy**, **planet**, **Solar System**.

△

The dark spots in Neptune's deep-blue atmosphere are probably storm regions.

neutron star

A neutron star is made up of tiny pieces of material. These tiny pieces, or particles, of **matter** are called neutrons. In a neutron star, the particles are packed tightly together. This makes the star very, very heavy. Just one teaspoonful of material from a neutron star would weigh millions of tonnes.

New Moon

See **phases of the Moon**.

Newton, Isaac

See **astronomy**.

night

Night is the time when your part of the Earth is dark. This is because it is facing away from the Sun. Night starts at sunset, when the Sun falls below the **horizon**. At night you can see the stars and planets shining in the dark sky. See also **day**, **time**.

northern lights

See **aurora**.

North Star

See **Polaris**.

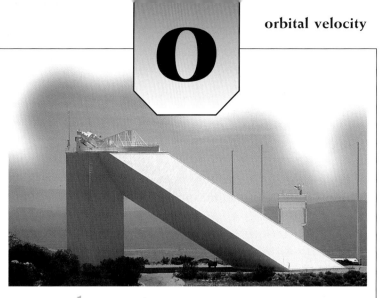

nova

A nova is a star that suddenly becomes very much brighter. To star-gazers on Earth, it may look as if a new star has appeared in the sky. The word 'nova' means new.
See also **supernova**.

nuclear reaction

When a nuclear reaction takes place, lots of energy is released. The energy is locked up inside the nucleus (centre) of **atoms**. The Sun and the stars use nuclear reactions to provide the energy to keep them shining. The process they use is called fusion. In fusion, light atoms join together to form a heavier atom.

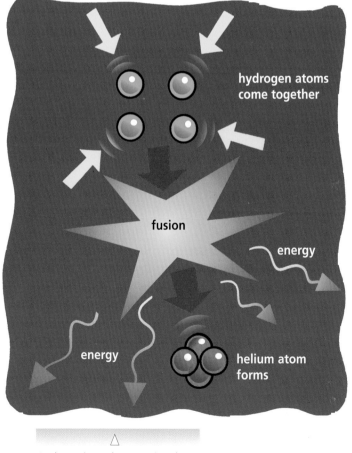

hydrogen atoms come together

fusion

energy

energy

helium atom forms

In the main nuclear reaction that takes place in stars, particles of hydrogen fuse (join) to form particles of helium.

observatory

An observatory is a place where astronomers work and study the stars and planets. In ordinary observatories, astronomers use telescopes to collect and study the light from the stars. These observatories are built high up on mountains where the air is clearer for viewing. At radio observatories, astronomers use **radio telescopes** to study the heavens.
See also **astronomy**.

open cluster

See **cluster**.

orbit

An orbit is the path that an object takes when it moves around another object in space. Earth and the other planets in the **Solar System** travel in orbits around the Sun. Satellites travel in orbits around Earth.

The shape of an orbit can be circular or elliptical (oval).

orbital velocity

The orbital velocity is the speed that a satellite must have to stay moving around. To stay in **orbit** 300 kilometres above the Earth, a satellite must have an orbital velocity of about 28,000 kilometres an hour. If a satellite's speed drops below orbital velocity, it will fall back to Earth.

orbiter

The orbiter is the main part of the space shuttle. It is the part that carries the crew and the payload, or cargo. It takes off from a launch pad like a rocket, but returns to Earth like a glider. It looks rather like a small aeroplane, but its wings are triangular in shape. There are four orbiters in the shuttle fleet: *Columbia*, *Discovery*, *Atlantis* and *Endeavour*. Another orbiter, called *Challenger*, was destroyed in a launching accident in 1986.

In the front of the orbiter is the crew cabin, which is supplied with air. It can carry up to eight astronauts. The cabin has two levels, or decks. On the upper deck is the cockpit, where the commander and pilot fly the craft. The crew have their living quarters on the deck below.

Behind the crew cabin is the payload bay, where the orbiter's cargo is stored. The bay is big enough to carry something as large as a railway carriage.

satellite

payload bay
living area
manoeuvring engines
heat shield

main
engines

satellite
launching
pod

The rocket engines are at the back of the orbiter. Its three main engines start firing on the launch pad. Their fuel comes from the big tank that is beneath the orbiter at lift-off.
See also **payload, space shuttle**.

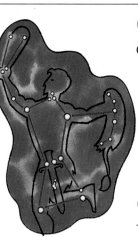

△

The imaginary figure of Orion, showing the hunter with his club raised up high.

△

A satellite is lifted from the payload bay of a space shuttle orbiter. The orbiter uses its robot arm to place the satellite in orbit.

Orion

Orion is one of the easiest patterns of stars to recognize. The **constellation** is supposed to show the figure of a male hunter. Bright stars mark his shoulders and legs, and three stars in the middle mark his belt. The hunter's sword contains the Orion Nebula.

Orion Nebula

The Orion Nebula is a very bright patch in the night sky. It is the brightest **nebula**. You can easily spot it with the naked eye in the constellation Orion. You will see it as a misty patch close to the three bright stars in the middle of the constellation. See also **Orion**.

Orion's Belt

See **Orion**.

oxidizer

See **propellant**.

△

Part of the Orion Nebula. It is a vast cloud of gas lit up by the light coming from nearby hot stars.

parsec

Professional astronomers use parsecs to measure distances in space. A more popular unit of measurement is the **light-year**. One parsec equals just over 3 light-years.

partial eclipse

See **eclipse**.

Pathfinder

See **Sojourner**.

It takes about 14 days for the Moon to go from a Full Moon (top) to a New Moon (bottom).

A satellite being carried by the space shuttle. It is the shuttle's payload. Soon it will be launched into space.

payload

The payload is the load that a spacecraft carries into space. Another name for payload is cargo. It can be a satellite, a probe, equipment for carrying out experiments, or parts of a space station. See also **Spacelab**.

period

A period is an amount of time. The period of a satellite is the time that it takes to travel round the Earth. A satellite that is 300 kilometres above the Earth has a period of about 1½ hours.

phases of the Moon

The Moon seems to change shape during each month. We call these different shapes the phases of the Moon. The Moon takes 29½ days to pass through all its phases, from one New Moon to the next.

You can see the Moon because it reflects light from the Sun. The phases happen because the Sun lights up different parts of the Moon. Sometimes the Sun lights up only the far side of the Moon. The side facing us stays dark, and we call this the New Moon. Slowly a thin slice, or crescent, of light appears. It grows bigger night after night. Eventually, all of the face of the Moon is lit up. We call this the Full Moon. If there are no clouds in the sky, the Full Moon casts shadows. As the nights go by we see less and less of the Moon lit up until it disappears at the next New Moon. See also **Harvest Moon, Moon**.

photosphere

See **Sun**.

Pioneer

Pioneer is the name of a group of American space probes. The best known are *Pioneer 10* and *11*. In 1973, *Pioneer 10* became the first probe to fly past Jupiter and take close-up pictures of it. *Pioneer 11* visited both Jupiter and Saturn. Both probes are now heading for the stars.

Pisces

See **zodiac**.

Planet

A planet moves in a circle around the Sun. There are nine planets altogether, including the planet that we live on – the Earth. The planets are part of the Sun's family, called the Solar System. They are kept in place in space by the Sun's enormous gravity (pull).

Each planet travels around the Sun along a path, or orbit, that never changes. The orbits, which are oval shaped, are very far apart.

You can see five of the planets with the naked eye: Mercury, Venus, Mars, Jupiter and Saturn. But you need a telescope to see Uranus, Neptune and Pluto. In the night sky, the planets always travel through the same constellations, or star patterns, each year. These are the constellations of the **zodiac**.

The planets are all very different. Some are large, others are small. Some are made up mainly of rock, others are made up mainly of gas. Some have no moons circling around them, and others have lots of moons. Some planets take only a few months to circle the Sun, but others take many years.
See also **Solar System**.

birth

The planets were born about 4600 million years ago. The Sun was formed at the same time. As the Sun became a glowing ball, a disc of matter formed around it. Bits of matter in the disc began to collide and form bigger lumps. These lumps slowly grew bigger and bigger until they became the planets.

Saturn looks beautiful when viewed through a telescope because of the shining rings that surround it.

brightness

At different times five of the planets are bright enough to be seen in the night sky. Three are easy to spot: Venus, Jupiter and Mars. Venus is by far the brightest. You can see it in the east or west at sunrise or sunset. Mercury and Saturn are dimmer and more difficult to spot. See also **evening star**, **morning star**.

'day'

Each planet spins round in space, just like the Earth does. A 'day' is the time that it takes to spin round once. Some planets spin faster than the Earth, others more slowly. Jupiter spins the fastest. Its 'day' lasts less than 10 hours.

distance

The distances between the planets are enormous. They are all a very long way away from Earth and from each other. Venus is the closest planet to Earth, yet it is more than 40 million kilometres away. Pluto, the most distant, lies more than 100 times farther away. It would take a jumbo jet over 600 years to reach Pluto!

gas giant

The planets Jupiter, Saturn, Uranus and Neptune are known as the gas giants. This is because they are huge when compared with Earth. Also, they are made up mainly of gas and liquid gas.

new planet

Until 1781, astronomers knew of only six planets. The farthest one they could see was Saturn. But in 1781, William Herschel in England discovered a new planet – Uranus. Astronomers then began to search for other new planets. In 1846 the German astronomer Johann Galle discovered Neptune. Finally, in 1930, the American astronomer Clyde Tombaugh discovered a ninth planet, Pluto. Some astronomers think there may be a tenth planet, Planet X.
See also **astronomy**.

▽

Many volcanoes are found on the surface of Venus. This one is called Maat Mons. It is as high as Mount Everest on Earth (8848 metres).

size

The planets are many different sizes. For example, Pluto is even smaller that our Moon, but Jupiter could swallow more than 1000 Earths. To get an idea of the different sizes of the planets, imagine them to be different kinds of fruit. If Earth were a grape, Venus would be a grape too. Pluto would be an apple pip, Mercury a blackcurrant and Mars a sultana. Uranus and Neptune would be grapefruits, Saturn a water melon and Jupiter a huge Hallowe'en pumpkin.

PLANET FACTS Planet	Diameter at equator (km)	Average distance from Sun (km)	No. of moons
Mercury	4,878	58,000,000	0
Venus	12,104	67,000,000	0
Earth	12,756	150,000,000	1
Mars	6,794	228,000,000	2
Jupiter	142,000	778,000,000	16
Saturn	120,000	1,427,000,000	23
Uranus	51,200	2,870,000,000	17
Neptune	49,500	4,497,000,000	8
Pluto	2,284	5,900,000,000	1

terrestrial planet

The terrestrial planets are the planets which are made up of rock, like Earth. They are sometimes called the rocky planets. These planets are Mercury, Venus and Mars. They are very much smaller than the four gas giants.

'year'

Each planet takes a certain time to travel once around the Sun. We call this time the planet's orbital period, or 'year'. The farther away the planet is from the Sun, the longer is its 'year'. The closest planet to the Sun, Mercury, takes only 88 days to circle the Sun. Pluto, the farthest planet, takes much longer to travel round the Sun. Its 'year' lasts almost 250 times longer than a year on Earth.

planetarium

A planetarium is a building where you can watch moving pictures of the night sky. The pictures are shown on the ceiling of a big domed room. With the help of computers, a planetarium can show you what it would be like to travel to distant stars, and what you would see when you arrived there.

planetary nebula

A planetary nebula is a round cloud of gas. It looks a bit like a planet. It forms when a dying star blows off layers of gas.
See also **nebula**.

The Pleiades star cluster contains as many as 200 stars altogether. They are all young and hot.

Pleiades

The Pleiades is a well-known group of stars. It is an example of an open **cluster**. It is also called the Seven Sisters. You can easily see the Pleiades with the naked eye in the constellation Taurus. You might be able to see its seven brightest stars if you have good eyesight.

Plough

The Plough is one of the best-known star patterns in the night sky. It is part of the constellation of Ursa Major, the Great Bear. The seven bright stars in the Plough look like the handle and blade of an old horse-drawn plough. The star pattern is also called the Big Dipper. See also **constellation**.

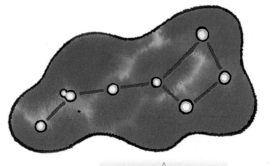

The Plough can be seen every night in most northern parts of the world.

This beautiful planetary nebula is called the Cat's Eye. The dying star that puffed out this cloud of gas can be seen in the centre.

Pluto P

Pluto is the smallest planet in the Solar System. It is usually the most distant planet from Earth. Pluto is a very cold planet, which is probably made up of rock and ice. It is only about half the size of our Moon. Its moon, Charon, is half the size of Pluto.
See also **Charon**, **planet**, **Solar System**.

Polaris

Polaris is a star that lies almost directly above the Earth's North Pole. The star is also called the North Star, or the Pole Star. Polaris does not appear to move as the Earth spins round on its **axis**. All the other stars appear to move through the night sky.

poles

The poles are points on the surface of a body in space, for example a planet. They lie on an imaginary line called the **axis**. The body spins around its axis.

Pole Star

See **Polaris**.

Pollux

See **star**.

probe

A probe is a spacecraft that travels beyond Earth. It escapes from the pull of Earth's **gravity**. Probes are sent to explore the Moon, planets, asteroids and comets. They take pictures and collect data (information) and send them back to Earth. Probes have now visited all the planets in the **Solar System** except Pluto.
See also **Galileo**, **Giotto**, **Mariner**, **Moon probe**, **Sojourner**, **Venera**, **Viking**, **Voyager**.

Procyon

See **star**.

prominence

A prominence is a fountain of glowing gas that shoots up from the surface of the Sun. From Earth, we can only see prominences during a total **eclipse** of the Sun.

Bright pink prominences show up around the edge of the Sun during a total eclipse.

propellant

A rocket burns propellants to make it go. Every rocket has two kinds of propellant: a fuel and a substance called an oxidizer. The oxidizer provides oxygen to burn the fuel. A common fuel used in rockets is liquid hydrogen, and a common oxidizer is liquid oxygen. Although these propellants are normally gases, they turn into liquids when cool enough.
See also **rocket**.

Proxima Centauri

Proxima Centauri is the nearest star to Earth. It is a small red star in the constellation Centaurus. It is about 40 million million kilometres, or 4.3 **light-years**, from Earth.

Ptolemy

See **astronomy**.

pulsar

A pulsar is a kind of tiny star. It sends out rapid pulses (bursts) of energy. This energy may be light rays or another type of **radiation**. Astronomers think that pulsars are rapidly spinning **neutron stars**. They beam pulses in our direction every time they spin round.

spinning neutron star

flash of light

Pulsars flash their beams into space rather like a lighthouse flashes its beams of light in the dark.

Q R

quasar

A quasar shines very brightly like an ordinary star, but it is too far away to be one. The name quasar is short for 'quasi-stellar', which means star-like. Astronomers think that quasars are a form of active galaxy.
See also **galaxy**.

A quasar shines brightly at the centre of a distant galaxy.

radar

On Earth, radar is used to find the positions of ships and aircraft. It is a method of sending out beams of radio waves, and receiving back echoes from anything in their path. In space, radar is used to study the surface of planets.

The Magellan *space probe used radar to study the surface of Venus. The radar could 'see' through the thick clouds that cover the planet.*

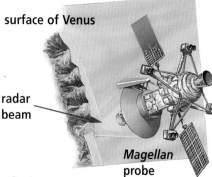

surface of Venus

radar beam

Magellan probe

radiation

Radiation means rays. The Sun and the stars give off radiation when they shine. They give off many kinds of radiation, such as light rays, which you can see, and other rays that are invisible. The invisible rays include infrared (heat) rays, ultraviolet (UV) rays, X-rays, gamma rays and radio waves.
See also **cosmic rays**.

radio galaxy

A radio galaxy is a group of stars that gives out large amounts of energy. It gives out most of its energy as radio waves. It is a kind of active galaxy.
See also **galaxy**.

radio telescope

A radio telescope collects radio signals from outer space. From these signals, astronomers produce pictures of the heavens. Most radio telescopes use a huge metal dish to pick up the signals. The biggest radio telescope, at Arecibo in Puerto Rico, has a dish that measures 305 metres across.

Ranger

Ranger is the name of a series of US probes that visited the Moon. They sent back the first close-up pictures of the Moon's surface in 1964.

The radio telescope at Parkes, New South Wales, Australia. Its dish is 64 metres across.

red giant

A red giant is a large red star. A star swells up and becomes a red giant when it begins to die. Red giants are much bigger than the Sun.

Red Planet

See **Mars**.

red shift

When light from the stars becomes redder we call this change red shift. The stars are moving away from us all the time. The change in colour happens because the light waves from the stars are stretched out as they move away.

re-entry

Re-entry is the moment when a spacecraft comes back into the air around the Earth. It re-enters the Earth's **atmosphere**.
See also **heat shield**.

relativity

The theory of relativity is a complicated set of ideas about space, time, energy and matter. The ideas were put forward by a German scientist, Albert Einstein, in the early 1900s.

S

remote-sensing satellite

See **satellite**.

retrorocket

A retrorocket is a rocket that slows down a spacecraft. It acts as a brake. It is fired in the opposite direction to which the spacecraft is travelling. The space shuttle fires retrorockets to slow down before it drops back down towards Earth.

Rigel

See **star**.

ring system

A ring system is a group of rings around a planet. There are rings of material around all the giant planets in the Solar System. See also **Saturn, shepherd moon**.

rocket

A rocket is a kind of engine. It provides the power to launch spacecraft. A rocket burns fuel to produce a jet of gases. The gases escape out of the rocket through a nozzle. As they shoot out backwards, the rocket shoots forwards.

Rockets work in space because they carry both fuel and the oxygen that is needed to burn the fuel. The fuel and the oxygen are different kinds of **propellant**. Most rockets burn liquid chemicals as propellants. In the future, spacecraft may be powered by rockets that send out streams of tiny pieces of matter or powerful light beams.
See also **launch vehicle, propellant**.

rocky planet

See **planet**.

Sagittarius

See **zodiac**.

▷ Saturn has a very beautiful ring system, which is made up of thousands of separate ringlets.

fuel tank

oxidizer tank

pump

combustion chamber

hot gases

◁ In a space rocket, liquid fuel and oxidizer (oxygen-provider) are burned in a chamber to produce a jet of gases.

Salyut

Salyut is the name of several Russian space stations. The first one went into orbit in 1971. The most successful of these stations were *Salyut 6* and *Salyut 7*. Cosmonauts stayed in these space stations for months at a time.

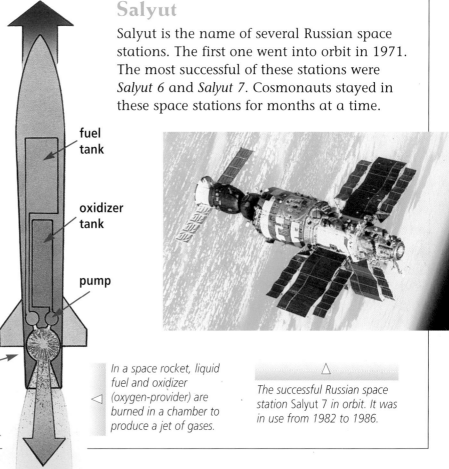

△
The successful Russian space station Salyut 7 in orbit. It was in use from 1982 to 1986.

Small moons circle around most of the planets in the Solar System. These moons are called natural satellites. The Earth has only one natural satellite, the Moon. But it has hundreds of man-made objects, or artificial satellites, circling round it. Usually we just call them satellites.

Satellites have become very important in the modern world. For example, we use them for sending television pictures around the world and for weather forecasting. They are also very important for astronomers, mapmakers and navigators, and they help us to watch over the Earth's environment.

Some satellites are tiny; others are huge. The Hubble Space Telescope, for example, is as big as a bus and weighs 11 tonnes. But whether they are big or small, all satellites have some things in common. They are built of lightweight materials such as aluminium. They carry a number of measuring instruments, cameras, aerials and a radio. The radio sends back measurements and images (pictures) as coded signals. Satellites are powered by electricity. This is made by panels of tiny **solar cells**.

Satellites circle hundreds of kilometres up in space, far above the Earth's **atmosphere**. They travel in their path, or orbit, at a very high speed, called their **orbital velocity**. If a satellite slows down too much, it will fall back to Earth. When it reaches the atmosphere, it burns up like a **meteor**. See also **telemetry**.

The Bay of Naples, in Italy, pictured by the remote-sensing satellite ERS-1. The colours in the photograph are false (not true).

astronomy satellite

Astronomy satellites carry telescopes and other instruments to look at the stars and planets. They study the heavens from above the Earth's atmosphere. Their instruments may pick up light or invisible rays such as X-rays. The Hubble Space Telescope picks up light. Infrared telescopes, like IRAS and ISO, pick up invisible infrared rays.

The large panels on this satellite have solar cells to supply electricity. Foil covers the satellite's body to protect it from the Sun's heat.

communications satellite

Communications satellites pass on signals from place to place. These signals are communications such as telephone calls, fax messages, e-mail, radio and TV programmes, and computer data (information). The communications are changed into coded signals. Most international communications pass through a network of **Intelsat** satellites.

environmental satellite

Environmental satellites keep watch over the Earth's environment. They measure such things as the amounts of polluting gases in the atmosphere. These gases may, for example, increase the **greenhouse effect**. They may also damage the layer of ozone gas that helps to protect Earth from dangerous rays from space.

navigation satellite

Navigation satellites help sailors, pilots and other travellers to find their way on land, at sea and in the air. The most widely used system of navigation satellites is called the Global Positioning System. It uses a network of 24 satellites, which beam out accurate signals telling people what their position is.

remote-sensing satellite

Remote-sensing satellites send back pictures of the Earth's surface. They are sometimes called Earth-resources satellites. The American Landsat and European ERS are examples of remote-sensing satellites. They take images (pictures) using different-coloured light. The images look quite different from ordinary photographs. They show up details that cannot be seen in ordinary photographs.

search and rescue satellite

Search and rescue satellites pick up emergency signals from boats or planes that are in trouble. The satellites are fitted with special equipment to pick up the signals. They save many people's lives every year.

weather satellite

Weather satellites send back the pictures you see on television weather forecasts. They also send back other weather data (information). These data include the temperature and humidity (amount of moisture) of the air. Some satellites, such as the NOAA ones, cover the whole world. Others, like Meteosat, just cover certain continents.

Shuttle astronauts capture a faulty satellite. Later, they will repair the satellite and launch it back into space.

Saturn ♄

Saturn is the second biggest planet in the Solar System, after Jupiter. It is more than ten times bigger across than Earth. The planet is made up mainly of gas and liquid gas. The most striking feature about Saturn is its system of shining rings. They are made up of millions of bits of ice and rock that whizz round at high speed. Saturn has more moons than any other planet – at least 23.
See also **aurora, planet, ring system, Solar System, Titan**.

This picture of Saturn shows displays of auroras in the north and south. They are similar to the northern and southern lights on Earth.

Saturn V

Saturn V was the huge rocket that sent the Apollo spacecraft to the Moon. It stood 111 metres tall and weighed about 3000 tonnes. It was designed by a team led by Wernher von Braun.
See also **Apollo spacecraft, exploring space, rocket**.

Scorpius

See **zodiac**.

sea (on the Moon)

The seas on the Moon are the dark patches that you can see on its surface. But they are not seas, because there is no water on the Moon. They are really large flat plains. Early astronomers called them *maria*, the Latin word for seas (*mare* is the word for a sea).
See also **Moon**.

season

A season is a time of the year on Earth with a certain pattern of weather. In many parts of the world there are four seasons: spring, summer, autumn and winter. The changes between the different seasons happen because of the way the Earth's **axis** is tilted in space either towards or away from the Sun. The planet Mars has seasons too.
See also **equinox, solstice**.

SETI

SETI is short for 'search for extraterrestrial intelligence'. This means looking for signs of intelligent living things somewhere else in space. Some astronomers use powerful **radio telescopes** to listen for radio signals that might be sent out by other intelligent beings.
See also **alien**.

A view of one of the Moon's seas called the Ocean of Storms. The large crater in the picture is Eratosthenes.

Seven Sisters

See **Pleiades**.

shepherd moon

A shepherd moon is a tiny moon near the rings around a planet. It helps to keep the pieces of the rings in place. See also **ring system**.

shooting star

See **meteor**.

shuttle

See **space shuttle**.

simulator

A simulator is a machine that astronauts use for training. US astronauts train in a space shuttle simulator. The inside of the simulator looks just like a real space shuttle. But when the astronauts practise a lift-off in the simulator, it stays on the ground.

Sirius

Sirius is the brightest star that you see in the sky. It is also called the Dog Star because it is in the constellation Canis Major (Great Dog). See also **star**.

Skylab

Skylab was an early US space station. It went into orbit in 1973.
Three teams of astronauts visited *Skylab* over a period of 10 months.
See also **exploring space**.

Astronauts flew up to Skylab in Apollo spacecraft. One of the space station's solar panels was ripped off at launch.

Small Magellanic Cloud

See **Magellanic Clouds**.

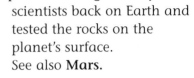
The robot vehicle Sojourner found out what Martian rocks are made of.

Sojourner

Sojourner was a vehicle that explored the planet Mars in 1997. It was carried there by the US *Pathfinder* probe. It was guided by scientists back on Earth and tested the rocks on the planet's surface.
See also **Mars**.

solar

Solar means to do with the Sun. A solar eclipse is an eclipse of the Sun.

solar cell

A solar cell is a tiny electric battery that turns sunlight into electricity. Most satellites are powered by solar panels that carry thousands of solar cells. The cells are made from thin slices of a material called silicon.

Two panels of solar cells supply electricity to the Hubble Space Telescope.

solar eclipse

See **eclipse**.

solar flare

See **flare**.

solar panel ripped off

solar telescopes

Apollo spacecraft

Solar System

The Solar System is the family of the Sun. It is made up of the Sun and the many different bodies that circle around it. The main bodies are the nine planets, which include Earth. Many of these planets have moons, like the Earth's Moon. Other bodies in the Solar System include **asteroids**, **comets** and **meteors**.
See also **planet, Sun**.

Soyuz

Soyuz is the name of the spacecraft that carry Russian cosmonauts into space. They have been flying since 1967. The cosmonauts return to Earth inside a round capsule, which lands safely with the help of parachutes.

▷ *Soyuz spacecraft have been carrying Russian cosmonauts into orbit for more than 30 years.*

Neptune • Sun • Jupiter • Earth • Uranus • Mercury • Mars • Venus • Saturn • Pluto

△
In the Solar System, the planets all circle around the Sun in the same direction.

solar wind

A solar wind is a stream of tiny pieces of matter from the Sun. The tiny pieces are called particles. When the wind reaches the Earth, it can cause **auroras.**

space

Space is the emptiness between the stars and planets. Most of the Universe is made up of empty space. Around the Earth, space begins above the **atmosphere**, at a height of about 300 kilometres.

solstice

A solstice is a time of year when the Sun is at its highest or its lowest point in the sky at midday. At the summer solstice the Sun rises to its highest point in the sky. In the northern half of the world this is on or near 21 June. At the winter solstice (on or near 21 December in the northern half of the world) the Sun reaches its lowest point in the sky at midday. In the southern half of the world the summer and winter solstices are the other way round.
See also **season**.

▽
Astronauts and scientists carry out all kinds of experiments in Spacelab.

spacecraft

A spacecraft is a machine that travels into space. The two main kinds of spacecraft are satellites and probes. Satellites circle round the Earth, while probes travel to distant planets, moons and comets.
See also **probe, satellite**.

Southern Cross

See **Crux**.

southern lights

See **aurora.**

Spacelab

Spacelab is a laboratory that is carried into space by the space shuttle. It stays in the **payload** bay of the shuttle all the time. Spacelab was built by the European Space Agency and first flew in November 1993.

spaceport

A spaceport is a major launching site for spacecraft. The world's busiest spaceports are the Kennedy Space Center in Florida, USA, and the Baikonur Cosmodrome in the republic of Kazakhstan, Central Asia. The Baikonur Cosmodrome is the main launching site for Russian spacecraft, such as Soyuz.
See also **Kennedy Space Center**.

space probe

See **probe**.

space shuttle

The space shuttle carries astronauts into space. It is the main launch vehicle used by NASA. Parts of the space shuttle can be re-used on other space flights. The shuttle is made up of three main parts. The **orbiter** carries the crew. The external tank holds the fuel for the orbiter's engines. The solid rocket **boosters**, or SRBs, provide extra power at lift-off. Both the orbiter and the SRBs are used again and again. The first shuttle flight took place on 12 April 1981.
See also **exploring space**.

△
The shuttle orbiter Discovery uses a parachute for braking as soon as it has landed.

space sickness

Most astronauts suffer from space sickness when they first arrive in space. They feel dizzy and sweaty, they have headaches and are often sick. They usually recover after two or three days when they get used to **weightlessness**.

space station

A space station is a large spacecraft in which astronauts live and work for months at a time. Cosmonauts have stayed on *Mir*, Russia's space station, for more than a year at a time. NASA is building an international space station. Europe, Japan, Russia and Canada are taking part in the project. It should be ready in 2002.
See also **Mir, Skylab**.

spacesuit

Astronauts wear a spacesuit when they go outside their spacecraft. It gives them oxygen to breathe and protects them from the heat and cold. It also protects them from any dangerous rays in outer space.

△
These two cosmonauts are wearing the underwear that they put on under their spacesuits. Water is passed through little tubes in the underwear to keep the cosmonauts cool.

space walk

See **extravehicular activity**.

Spica

See **star**.

splashdown

Splashdown is the moment when a spacecraft falls into the sea after a space flight.

Sputnik 1

Sputnik 1 was the world's first spacecraft. It was a **satellite** that circled the Earth. *Sputnik 1* was launched by Russia. It went into orbit around the Earth on 4 October 1957.
See also **exploring space**.

Every night when the Sun sets, the sky grows dark. If it is clear, you can watch the stars appear. There are more stars in the Universe than any other object. The stars look tiny in the sky because they are so far away. Even their light takes many years to reach us. They are in the sky during the day as well. But you cannot see them because the sky is too bright.

When you look up at the starry sky, it seems as if the stars are stuck onto the inside of a huge dark ball. During the night, the stars move slowly overhead as if the ball is spinning around the Earth. Ancient astronomers believed in this ball, and called it the **celestial sphere**. In fact there is no celestial sphere. The stars above move because the Earth is spinning round in space.

You can find your way around the night sky by looking at the patterns of bright stars. We call these patterns the **constellations**. Millions of stars group together to make huge star islands called **galaxies**. Between the galaxies there is empty space.

If you could travel near to a star, it would be like the Sun. This is because the Sun itself is a star. It is a great ball of very hot gas, which gives off light that you can see and heat that you can feel. All stars are like this.

birth

A star is born in a great cloud of gas and dust in space. We call these clouds **nebulas**. A star starts to form when part of a nebula begins to shrink. In time, it shrinks into a ball shape and heats up. The smaller it gets, the hotter it becomes. One day it becomes so hot that it starts to shine brightly as a new star.
See also **brown dwarf**.

brightness

Some stars are brighter than others in the night sky. The brightness of a star as you see it does not tell you how bright the star really is. This is because all the stars lie at different distances from us. And the farther away a star is, the dimmer it appears to our eyes. So a very dim star nearby can appear brighter than a very bright star very far away.
See also **magnitude**.

colour

Although the stars seem to be white, they really have different colours. In the constellation Orion, for example, Rigel is brilliant white and Betelgeuse quite orange. There are also many bluish, yellowish and reddish stars. Bluish-white stars are the hottest stars, and reddish stars are the coolest.

companion

Some stars travel through space together with one or more companion stars. Others travel on their own. In a star **cluster**, hundreds and sometimes hundreds of thousands of stars may travel together.
See also **double star**.

Great clouds of gas and dust billow out from one of the biggest stars we know, called Eta Carinae.

A star like the Sun shines steadily for a long time. Then it swells into a red giant, before shrinking into a white dwarf.

nebula

planetary nebula

solar-type star

red giant

white dwarf

death

One day all the stars will die and fade away. This will not happen for many millions of years. When a very big star dies, it first swells up into a **supergiant** and then blasts itself apart in a **supernova** explosion. Afterwards, all that is left is a tiny **neutron star** or a **black hole**.
See also **red giant**, **white dwarf**.

energy

A star needs huge amounts of energy to keep shining. This energy is made deep inside the star by **nuclear reactions**. The star gives off this energy as rays of light and heat, as well as invisible rays such as X-rays.
See also **radiation**.

movement

All the stars are moving rapidly through space. You cannot see most stars move because they are too far away. With a telescope you can see a few of the nearest stars move slightly as the years go by. The stars also move in another way. They spin round in space, just like the Earth does.

size

Stars come in many different sizes. Many are the same size as the Sun, which is more than 100 times bigger across than the Earth. But the Sun is a dwarf, or small star. **White dwarfs** are even smaller. In contrast, we know of many stars that are hundreds of millions of kilometres across. We call these stars **supergiants**.
See also **neutron star**.

twinkling

When you look at the stars, their brightness seems to be changing all the time. They seem to be twinkling slightly. In fact the stars shine steadily. The twinkling effect is caused by moving air in the Earth's **atmosphere**.

name	constellation	magnitude
Sirius	Canis Major	−1.5
Canopus	Carina	−0.7
Alpha Centauri	Centaurus	−0.2
Arcturus	Boötes	−0.1
Vega	Lyra	0.0
Capella	Auriga	0.1
Rigel	Orion	0.1
Procyon	Canis Minor	0.4
Achernar	Eridanus	0.5
Beta Centauri	Centaurus	0.6
Altair	Aquila	0.8
Betelgeuse	Orion	0.8
Aldebaran	Taurus	0.9
Acrux	Crux	0.9
Spica	Virgo	1.0
Antares	Scorpius	1.0
Pollux	Gemini	1.2
Fomalhaut	Piscis Austrinus	1.2
Deneb	Cygnus	1.3
Mimosa	Crux	1.3

△
The table lists the 20 brightest stars you can see in the sky. The last column shows their magnitude, which tells you how bright they are.

▷ The Sun is much bigger than the stars we call red dwarfs and white dwarfs. But astronomers call the Sun a dwarf too. Many stars are hundreds of times bigger.

white dwarf

red dwarf

Sun

star map

Astronomers use star maps to find their way around the night sky. Modern maps show the position of stars very accurately.

star sign

See **astrology**.

The Sun is a boiling mass of gases. Its temperature is about 5500 degrees Celsius. The dark sunspots that appear on its surface are cooler.

stellar

Stellar means to do with the stars. The stellar Universe means the Universe of stars.

step rocket

See **launch vehicle**.

Summer Triangle

In the summer in the northern half of the world, three bright stars appear high overhead. They make up the Summer Triangle. The stars are Deneb (in the constellation Cygnus), Vega (in Lyra) and Altair (in Aquila).
See also **star**.

Sun

The Sun is an ordinary star. It gives the Earth its light and warmth. The Sun looks so much bigger and brighter than the other stars because it is much closer to Earth. It lies about 150,000,000 kilometres away. The other stars lie millions and millions of kilometres away.

The Sun is made up of hot glowing gas that gives out a yellowish light. It is quite a small star, and astronomers call it a yellow dwarf. But if you compare the Sun with the Earth, it is enormous. The Sun measures about 1,400,000 kilometres across. It could swallow a million bodies the size of Earth.
See also **eclipse**, **flare**, **Solar System**, **solar wind**, **star**, **sunspot**.

This early star map is beautifully illustrated with figures of the constellations.

sunspot

A sunspot is a dark patch on the surface of the Sun. It looks dark because it is cooler than the surrounding area. Sunspots come and go regularly over a period of about 11 years. This is called the sunspot cycle.

supergiant

A supergiant is the biggest and brightest kind of star. It is many hundreds of times bigger and brighter than the Sun. Usually, supergiants blow themselves apart in a **supernova** explosion.
See also **star**.

The surface of the Sun is stormy. Great fountains of flaming gas often shoot out, and then loop back again. Astronomers call them prominences.

supernova

A supernova is a star that suddenly becomes very bright. This happens when the star explodes and blasts itself apart. For a time the supernova shines more brightly than all the other stars in its galaxy put together. In February 1987 astronomers spotted the brightest supernova for over 300 years – it was named SN 1987A.

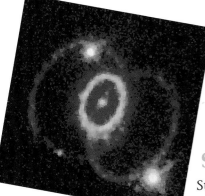

◁ *Rings of glowing gas are now found where supernova SN 1987A exploded. They will expand (grow bigger) as time goes by.*

Surveyor

Surveyor is the name of a series of US probes that landed on the Moon. The first Surveyor landed there in 1966. The probes sent back photographs and dug into the Moon's surface to test the soil.

△ *Most professional astronomers use mirror telescopes, or reflectors, and work in observatories. The telescopes are housed in giant domes, with roofs that open at night. They are fixed to movable mountings (stands) so that they can be pointed to any part of the sky.*

Taurus

See **zodiac**.

telemetry

Telemetry is the sending back of signals by radio from spacecraft to Earth. The signals carry measurements from scientific instruments as well as information about how the spacecraft is working.

telescope

Astronomers use telescopes to see far into space. The word 'telescope' means seeing far. It is the main instrument that astronomers use to study the heavens. Ordinary light telescopes collect the light from stars and planets with lenses or mirrors. **Radio telescopes** collect the radio waves that these bodies give out.

A telescope with lenses is called a refracting telescope, or a refractor. A large lens at the front collects the light and forms an image (picture). You look at the image through a lens next to your eye, called the eyepiece. The lenses are inside tubes that you can slide backwards and forwards to focus (make a clear image).

▽ *This diagram shows the path of light through a lens telescope, or refractor. Many amateur astronomers use refractors.*

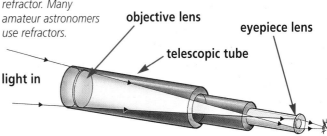

objective lens

eyepiece lens

telescopic tube

light in

A telescope that uses mirrors to collect light is called a reflecting telescope, or a reflector. All the biggest telescopes in the world are reflectors. Some have mirrors up to 10 metres across. A large curved mirror collects the light from the stars and reflects it onto another mirror. This second mirror reflects the light into an eyepiece at the side of the telescope or behind the main mirror.

See also **astronomy, astrophotography**.

Tereshkova, Valentina

See **exploring space**.

terrestrial

Terrestrial means to do with the Earth. The terrestrial planets are the rocky planets like Earth.
See also **planet**.

thruster

A thruster is a small rocket engine. Spacecraft fire thrusters to move around once they are up in space.

As the Moon circles the Earth, its gravity tugs at the sea beneath. It makes the sea level rise, causing a high tide. On either side, the water is pulled away from the land, causing a low tide.

low tide

Earth

high tide

pull of the Moon

pull of the Sun

tide

A tide is the movement of the sea towards or away from the land. Twice each day the sea flows in to a high point (high tide) and out to a low point (low tide). Tides are caused mainly by the Moon's **gravity**, which pulls on the water in the sea. The pull of the Sun's gravity affects the height of tides, causing very high tides at certain times of the year.

time

The kind of time we use everyday is called solar time. It is based on the movement of the Earth in relation to the Sun. For example, one day is the time Earth takes to spin round once.

In astronomy, time is based on the movement of the Earth in relation to the stars. This kind of time is called sidereal time. One sidereal day is the time between when a star rises one day and the next. It is about four minutes shorter than a normal day.
See also **day**, **season**, **year**.

Titan

Titan is the largest moon of Saturn. It is the second largest moon in the whole Solar System. Titan measures 5140 kilometres across, and is half as big again as our own Moon. The interesting thing about Titan is that it is the only moon that has an **atmosphere**.
See also **moon**, **Saturn**.

total eclipse

See **eclipse**.

tracking

Tracking means following the path of a spacecraft through space. Tracking stations use huge dish aerials to receive the signals that spacecraft give out.

trajectory

The trajectory is the flight path of a rocket or spacecraft through space.

Galileo

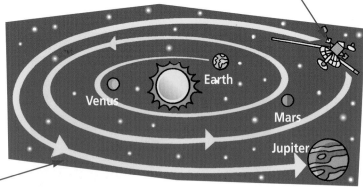

Galileo's trajectory

Venus

Earth

Mars

Jupiter

Tsiolkovsky, Konstantin

See **exploring space**.

The probe Galileo followed a great looping trajectory on its way to Jupiter.

Tycho

Tycho is a large crater on the surface of the Moon. It is easy to spot at the time of the Full Moon, when you can see it towards the south of the Moon. It is surrounded by shining white **crater rays**.
See also **phases of the Moon**.

U

UFO

UFO is short for unidentified flying object. It means something in the sky that cannot easily be explained. Many people claim they have seen UFOs that are shaped like saucers. Some people imagine that these 'flying saucers' are spaceships from another world. But there is no proof that they are. Many UFOs turn out to be high-flying aircraft, weather balloons or bright planets, like Venus.

ultraviolet rays

See **radiation**.

△

This picture shows a UFO that people said hovered over the city of Shiogama, in Japan, in 1986.

Ulysses

Ulysses was a European space probe that studied the poles of the Sun for the first time. It made its observations in 1994 and 1995. *Ulysses* travelled to the Sun by way of Jupiter.

Universe

The Universe is everything that exists. It is made up of space and **matter.** The matter takes the form of millions of galaxies, and each galaxy contains millions and millions of stars. The Universe appears to be getting bigger. Astronomers think that the Universe began with a **Big Bang** about 15,000 million years ago. It might carry on expanding for ever, or it might end in a **Big Crunch**.

▽

There is a faint ring system around Uranus. Spacecraft have spotted it, but it is difficult to see from Earth.

Uranus ☿

Uranus is a large and distant planet in the Solar System. It is made up mainly of gas. You cannot see it with the naked eye. It is about four times bigger across than Earth, and is similar in size to Neptune. Miranda is the strangest of its 15 moons. Neptune was not discovered until the 1700s.
See also **astronomy**, **Miranda**, **planet**, **Solar System**.

UV rays

See **radiation**.

▽

This 'deep field' picture was taken by the Hubble Space Telescope. It looks farther into the Universe than we have ever seen before.

V-2

See **exploring space**.

VAB

VAB is short for Vehicle Assembly Building. It is a giant building at the Kennedy Space Center in Florida, USA. The VAB, which is 210 metres long and 50 storeys high, was built to house the *Saturn V* rocket.

△

The huge VAB is now used to assemble the space shuttle.

Van Allen belts

The Van Allen belts are ring-shaped areas that surround the Earth. They give off large amounts of **radiation**. The belts are high up above the Earth's surface. They were discovered by the USA's first satellite, *Explorer 1*. The belts are named after a US scientist called James Van Allen.

variable star

A variable star changes to become brighter or dimmer. Some, like the Cepheids, really do change in brightness. Others are **double stars**. See also **Algol**.

Vega

See **star**.

Vehicle Assembly Building

See **VAB**.

Venera probes

Venera is the name of several Russian probes that explored the planet Venus. *Venera 10* was the first probe to land on Venus and take pictures of its surface, in 1975. See also **Venus**.

Venus ♀

Venus is the closest planet to Earth. It sometimes comes as close as 42 million kilometres. It is nearly the same size as Earth and has an **atmosphere**. But it is quite unlike the Earth in other ways. The temperature on the surface of Venus is over 450 degrees Celsius. This is hot enough to melt some metals. The planet is so hot because its thick atmosphere of carbon dioxide gas acts like a greenhouse.
See also **greenhouse effect**, **planet**, **Solar System**.

△

This large crater on Venus was made by a meteorite. The crater, called Howe, measures about 37 kilometres across.

Very Large Array

The Very Large Array is the world's biggest telescope. It is an example of a **radio telescope**. It is made up of 27 small dish aerials that can be moved into different positions along railway tracks.

Some of the aerials that make up the Very Large Array, near Socorro in New Mexico, USA.

Viking

Viking is the name of two American probes that explored Mars. They reached the planet in 1976. Each probe consisted of an orbiter and a lander. The orbiter took photographs of the planet from above. The lander photographed the surface, checked the weather, and looked for signs of life in the soil.

Virgo

See **zodiac**.

Virgo Cluster

The Virgo Cluster is the nearest large group of galaxies. It is found in the constellation Virgo, and contains several thousand galaxies.
See also **cluster**.

Von Braun, Wernher

See **exploring space**.

Vostok spacecraft

Vostok spacecraft carried the first cosmonauts into space. Human space flight began when *Vostok 1* carried Yuri Gagarin into space on 12 April 1961.
See also **exploring space**.

aerial →

nuclear battery

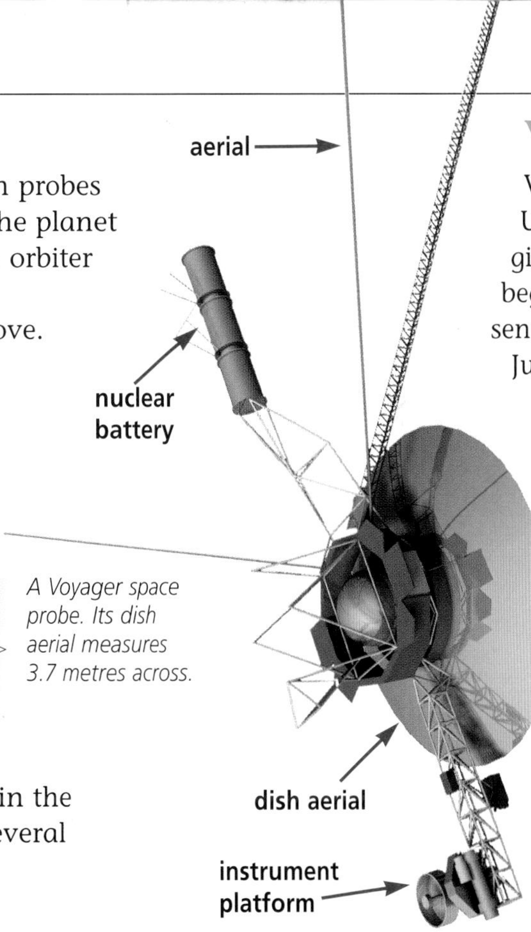

A Voyager space probe. Its dish aerial measures 3.7 metres across.

dish aerial

instrument platform

Voyager

Voyager is the name of two US probes that explored the giant planets. Their journey began in 1979. Both probes sent back detailed pictures of Jupiter and Saturn and their moons. *Voyager 2* went on to visit Uranus and Neptune, taking the first close-up pictures of these planets. Both probes are now heading for the stars.

Both Voyager probes carry recorded disks with messages from people on Earth. The disks also contain views and sounds of natural and man-made things found on Earth.
See also **exploring space, planet**.

W X Y Z

weather satellite

See **satellite**.

weightlessness

When astronauts travel in space, they feel as if their bodies have no weight. We call this condition weightlessness. In the weightless world of space, nothing falls if you drop it. It just stays where it is.
See also **free fall**.

△
Japanese astronaut Chiaki Mukai floats weightless in Spacelab while she goes to work.

white dwarf

A white dwarf is a tiny star that gives off white light. It is not much bigger than the Earth. A white dwarf is very dense (heavy) for its size. Just one teaspoonful of matter from it would weigh several tonnes.
See also **star**.

◁ *This X-15 rocket plane reached speeds of over 7000 kilometres per hour.*

▽ *The zodiac passes through 12 separate constellations. Most of them are named after animals.*

X plane

An X plane was a very fast rocket plane that could reach the edge of space. Many X planes climbed so high that their pilots were classed as astronauts.

X-rays

See **radiation**.

year

A year is the time that it takes for the Earth to travel once around the Sun. It is a basic unit of time. One year is equal to 365¼ days.
See also **day**, **time**.

zenith

The zenith is an imaginary point in the heavens directly above your head.

zero gravity

Zero-gravity, or zero-g for short, means no gravity. It is another term for **weightlessness**.

zodiac

The Sun, the Moon and the planets all seem to move through a broad band in the sky. We call it the zodiac. The word 'zodiac' means circle of animals.
See also **astrology**, **constellation**.

1. Aries
2. Taurus
3. Gemini
4. Cancer
5. Leo
6. Virgo
7. Libra
8. Scorpius
9. Sagittarius
10. Capricornus
11. Aquarius
12. Pisces

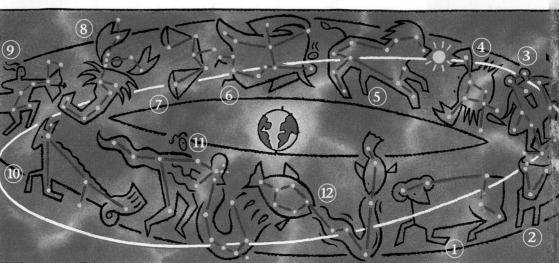